CASTRO'S
AMERICA DEPARTMENT

Coordinating Cuba's Support for
Marxist-Leninist Violence
in the Americas

By
Rex A. Hudson

The Cuban American National Foundation
1988

ABOUT THE AUTHOR

Rex A. Hudson is a Senior Research Specialist in Latin American affairs at the Library of Congress, Washington, D.C. He has published previous articles on Latin American political-military affairs in *Terrorism: An International Journal* and *Inter-American Economic Affairs*. A former Peace Corps Volunteer (Bolivia, 1970-71), he earned an M.A. in International Affairs from George Washington University.

An earlier version of this report was published in *Terrorism: An International Journal*, vol. 9, no. 2 (1987), pp. 125-167.

TABLE OF CONTENTS

List of Abbreviations i

Introduction 1

I.   Castro's Covert War 3

II.   The Guevarist Years 5

III.   Soviet-Cuban Rapprochement 10

IV.   The PCC/CC's "Guerrilla International" 17

V.   The Nicaraguan Revolutionary Model 23

VI.   Castro's Nicaraguan "Robot" 27

VII.   Exporting the Nicaraguan Model 34

       Central America 34

       The Caribbean 44

       South America 46

       The United States 56

VIII. DA/DGRE Foreign Policy Influence 60

IX.   The Soviet-Cuban Diplomatic Gambit 62

X.   Conclusion and Outlook 64

Appendix 1: Cited DA Officials 67

Appendix 2: Biographical Profile:
       Manuel Piñeiro Losada 69

Book References 71

LIST OF ABBREVIATIONS

AVC	Alfaro Lives [Ecuador]
CCGI	International Guerrilla Coordinating Committee
CEA	Center for North American Studies [DA, Cuba]
CEAL	Center for Latin American Studies [DA, Cuba]
CP	Communist Party
CPSU	Communist Party of the Soviet Union
CRN	National Revolutionary Command [Puerto Rico]
DA	America Department [Cuba]
DGI	General Directorate of Intelligence [Cuba]
DGRE	General Directorate of Foreign Relations [Cuba]
DGSE	General Directorate of State Security [Nicaragua]
DL	Liberation Directorate [Cuba]
DLN	National Liberation Directorate [Cuba]
DNU-MRH	National Unity Directorate of the Revolutionary Movement of Honduras
DOE	Special Operations Directorate [Cuba]
DRI	International Relations Department [Nicaragua]
DRU	Unified Revolutionary Directorate [El Salvador]
DSE	State Security Department [Cuba]
ELN	National Liberation Army [Bolivia]
ELN	National Liberation Army [Colombia]
EPL	Popular Liberation Army [Colombia]
EPS	Sandinista People's Army [Nicaragua]
ERP	People's Revolutionary Army [Argentina]
ERP	People's Revolutionary Army [El Salvador]
FALN	Armed Forces of National Liberation [Puerto Rico]
FALN	Armed Forces of National Liberation [Venezuela]
FARC	Revolutionary Armed Forces of Colombia
FARN	Armed Forces of National Resistance [El Salvador]
FBI	Federal Bureau of Investigation [United States]
FHLP	Honduran Front for Popular Liberation
FMLN	Farabundo Martí National Liberation Front [El Salvador]
FPMR	Manuel Rodríguez Popular Front [Chile]
FPR-LZ	Lorenzo Zelaya Popular Revolutionary Front [Honduras]

FSLN	Sandinista National Liberation Front [Nicaragua]
GCR	General Revolutionary Command [Guatemala]
ICAP	Institute for Friendship With the Peoples [Cuba]
JCR	Revolutionary Coordinating Junta
KGB	Committee for State Security [Soviet Union]
M-19	19th of April Movement [Colombia]
M-26	26th of July Movement [Cuba]
MININT	Interior Ministry [Cuba]
MINREX	Ministry of Foreign Relations [Cuba]
MINT	Ministry of Interior [Nicaragua]
MIR	Movement of the Revolutionary Left [Chile]
MLN	National Liberation Movement or Tupamaros [Uruguay]
MRN	New Republic Movement [Costa Rica]
MRTA	Tupac Amaru Revolutionary Movement [Peru]
NJM	New Jewel Movement [Grenada]
OAS	Organization of American States
OLAS	Latin American Solidarity Organization [Cuba]
OVRP	Organization of Volunteers for the Puerto Rican Revolution
PCC/CC	Communist Party of Cuba/Central Committee
PCCh	Communist Party of Chile
PCES	Communist Party of El Salvador
PDF	Panama Defense Forces
PFLP	Popular Front for the Liberation of Palestine
PLO	Palestine Liberation Organization
PSP	Puerto Rican Socialist Party
PVP	Popular Vanguard Party [Costa Rica]
RVP	People's Revolutionary Party [Suriname]
SI	Socialist International
SL	Shining Path [Peru]
UN	United Nations
URNG	Guatemalan National Revolutionary Union
WPJ	Workers Party of Jamaica

When I saw rockets firing...I swore to myself that the Americans were going to pay dearly for what they were doing. When this war is over, a much wider and bigger war will begin for me: the war that I'm going to launch against them. I am aware that this is my true destiny.

— Fidel Castro in a letter to his aide and
confidante Celia Sánchez in 1958[1]

INTRODUCTION

In 1985, Latin America surpassed Western Europe as the region with the most acts of international terrorism against U.S. targets, and remained a prime venue of domestic and international terrorist incidents in 1986 and 1987. Largely responsible for the steadily increasing levels of anti-American and anti-state violence in Latin America during the 1980s are at least two dozen Marxist-Leninist organizations known to receive support and advice from Cuba.

Pro-Cuban groups currently pose serious national security threats to two Latin American countries in particular, El Salvador and Colombia. In Colombia, many significant acts of anti-U.S. and anti-state terrorism also have been sponsored by the cocaine trafficking mafia known as the Medellín Cartel, which has hired the services of the Colombian guerrilla groups. Policy-makers should be particularly concerned about these dual threats to democratic governments in Latin America, as well as Cuban/Soviet-supported efforts to establish Marxist regimes in Panama and Chile.

It is doubtful that the Sandinista National Liberation Front (FSLN) could have seized power in Nicaragua in 1979 without Cuba's extensive material, advisory, and other support. The Sandinista victory vindicated the Cuban-Soviet "political-military" model of revolution which conditions Cuban-Soviet support for so-called "national liberation movements" on their progress in unifying in an alliance with the local pro-Soviet Communist party, through which Cuban guidance could then be provided. Since 1979, the Sandinista regime in Nicaragua has actively assisted Cuban efforts to support the extreme left in the region, and, therefore, policy-makers must also be equally concerned about Nicaragua's subversive activities.

---

[1] As cited by Herbert L. Matthews, *Fidel Castro* (New York: Simon & Schuster, 1969), p.121.

This paper will examine how and to what extent Cuba and Nicaragua have been supporting guerrilla warfare and terrorism by Marxist-Leninist organizations in the hemisphere since 1979. It will focus on the guerrilla and terrorist coordinating and support activities of the Cuban Communist Party Central Committee's (PCC/CC) America Department (DA), as well as the DA's counterpart organization in Nicaragua, the International Relations Directorate (DRI). These agencies—supported by a network of other organizations in their respective intelligence and security services—are responsible for conducting their governments' subversive programs in the hemisphere. Various Cuban and Nicaraguan intelligence defectors have emphasized, moreover, that Cuba controls the Nicaraguan intelligence and security apparatus and uses it as a front to obscure Havana's own covert activities in the region.

Some of the Castroite groups discussed in this paper—such as those in Argentina, Chile, Peru, and Honduras—are primarily urban terrorist organizations, without any significant guerrilla forces engaging in rural insurgency. These groups have not advanced sufficiently in their organizational development to wage a viable guerrilla insurgency. Others—such as those in El Salvador, Guatemala, and Colombia—may be categorized as primarily guerrilla organizations that engage in skirmishes with military and security forces and exercise de facto control over some territory in remote areas. Most of the Cuban-supported guerrilla groups, however, also systematically perpetrated terrorism, such as kidnap/ransom operations, in their formative years and continue using it selectively.

Castroite groups usually carry out actions consonant with Havana's strategic objectives and guidance, and the dictates of Marxism-Leninism, i.e., targeting representatives of Western democratic governments (especially the United States) and rightist dictatorships (namely Chile), and in solidarity with other Marxist-Leninist or pro-Soviet revolutionary groups or regimes (such as Libya) in other regions. The solidarity factor helps to explain why several Sandinista terrorists assisted the infamous hijacker Leila Khaled of the Popular Front for the Liberation of Palestine (PFLP) in an unsuccessful attempt to hijack an Israeli airliner in London in 1970, and why Colombian 19th of April (M-19) terrorists participated in the kidnapping of an Ecuadorean banker by an Ecuadorean terrorist group in 1985. This ideological solidarity is currently being demonstrated in Colombia and Panama, where Cubans, Nicaraguans, and members of foreign terrorist organizations are reportedly organizing international brigades to engage in guerrilla warfare or terrorism.

I. CASTRO'S COVERT WAR

A growing body of information provided by credible sources, including high-level Cuban and Nicaraguan intelligence defectors, contradicts compellingly the myth that after Ernesto "Ché" Guevara's defeat in Bolivia in 1967 Castro gave up "exporting revolution" to pursue a more "mature" policy of developing good state-to-state relations in Latin America.[2] For example, Pamela S. Falk noted in her well-documented textbook, *Cuban Foreign Policy*, that Castro has never abandoned "the policy of promoting revolution both by the expansion of diplomatic relations and armed struggle," a policy which "continued as a principal program in Cuban foreign policy from the early days of the revolution."[3] Jiri and Virginia Valenta have amply documented how Cuba, backed by the Soviet Union, "has played a pivotal role" in exacerbating local and regional problems "by assisting the revolutionary guerrilla movements."[4]

Although the basic causes of revolution clearly cannot be exported, Cuba—aided by Nicaragua since July 1979—has provided the catalysts needed to foment and support "armed struggle" in vulnerable countries of Latin America, e.g., through the provision of arms, munitions, and safehaven, as well as guerrilla and terrorist training and logistical, financial, propaganda, advisory and other support. Under Cuban guidance, these Castroite groups have pursued a systematic, graduated strategy for waging revolutionary terrorism

---

[2] For example, this myth is promoted in Carla Anne Robbins' *The Cuban Threat* (Philadelphia: ISHI Publications, 1985); Wayne S. Smith's *The Closest of Enemies: A Personal and Diplomatic Account of US-Cuban Relations Since 1957* (New York and London: W.W. Norton & Co., 1987); and Jorge I. Domínguez's "Cuba in the 1980s," *Foreign Affairs*, Fall 1986, p. 130. The thesis that Cuba's state-to-state relations have taken precedence over subversion and support of the left is also posited by Damian J. Fernández, *Cuba's Foreign Policy in the Middle East* (Boulder, Colorado: Westview, 1988.)

[3] Pamela S. Falk, *Cuban Foreign Policy: Caribbean Tempest* (Lexington, Mass.: Lexington Books, 1986), p. 24.

[4] Jiri and Virginia Valenta, "Soviet Strategies and Policies in the Caribbean Basin," in Wiarda, Howard J. and Mark Falcoff, eds., *The Communist Challenge in the Caribbean and Central America* (Washington, D.C.: American Enterprise Institute, 1987), p. 79. This essay is essential reading for a comprehensive overview of Soviet-Cuban activities in the region.

against the U.S. presence and local government and military officials.

As noted above, the trends in Latin America in recent years indicate growing levels of anti-U.S. Castroite and Maoist terrorism and acts of guerrilla sabotage, such as oil pipeline bombings against American petroleum companies in Colombia. According to the U.S. State Department, Latin America accounted for about fifty-five percent of all incidents of terrorism involving U.S. targets in 1986. With 159 international terrorist attacks, or one-third more than in 1985, Latin America replaced Western Europe that year as the second most active arena for international terrorism. Most of the 1986 incidents took place in Colombia, Peru, and Chile.[5] In 1987, Latin America continued to be by far the leading region of anti-U.S. terrorist incidents.

Castro has indeed fulfilled the pledge he made in a July 26, 1960, speech to convert the Andes into the Sierra Maestra of all America. Today, Castroite groups pose significant guerrilla or terrorist threats in the larger Pacific Coast Andean countries—Chile, Peru, and Colombia—as well as Central America. The PCC/CC's DA has worked quietly and effectively to train, build up, and unify at least twenty-seven active guerrilla organizations that are operating in many countries of the region and—in late 1987—totaled about 25,000 armed and trained members.[6] According to the U.S. Southern Command (Southcom), all of these groups—with the main exception of the Maoist Shining Path (SL) in Peru—are Marxist-Leninist and known to be supported by Cuba.[7] Southcom and U.S. State Department analysts have estimated that a minimum of 20,000 individuals from around the world, including more than 10,000 Latin Americans, have attended at least one of the more than fifty guerrilla or terrorist training courses offered in Cuban military facilities since Castro seized power in 1959.[8] Between the mid-1970s and mid-1980s, an additional 20,000 individuals from several African countries and Nicaragua had

[5] U.S. Department of State, *Patterns of Global Terrorism: 1986*, October 1987, pp. 1, 3, 24-25.

[6] Richard Halloran, "Latin Guerrillas Joining Forces, U.S. Officers Say," *New York Times*, March 3, 1987; and "Guerrilla Forces '25,000 Strong'," *Latin American Weekly Report*, November 5, 1987, p. 5, citing an 'exclusive' briefing by U.S. Southcom senior officers.

[7] *Ibid.*

[8] *Ibid.*; and U.S. Department of State, Bureau of Public Affairs, *Soviet Activities in Latin America and the Caribbean*, Current Policy No. 669, February 28, 1985.

undergone indoctrination at Cuba's Isle of Youth "educational" complex.[9]

After two decades of trial and error, Castro, with the aid of the DA, finally found the right formula for revolution in Nicaragua in 1979. Convinced that the "Nicaraguan model" could be replicated elsewhere, the DA has been working relentlessly ever since to coordinate and systematize similar efforts throughout Latin America. The DA has selectively provided material, training, and advisory support for "armed struggle" from San Juan and San Salvador to Santiago. By using Cuba's diplomatic missions and other fronts, including Nicaragua itself, the DA has expertly cloaked its own key role, allowing Castro to simultaneously improve Cuba's diplomatic standing in the region. Cuba's so-called "mature" image has, in turn, permitted the Soviet Union to make significant diplomatic gains in Latin America.

This report will trace the evolution of the DA, as well as the expansion of its role and influence in helping to develop and implement the Cuban-Soviet "political-military" revolutionary strategy in the hemisphere, at least insofar as these activities have been reported by journalists, scholars, a 1981 U.S. Department of State report, and Cuban and Nicaraguan intelligence defectors. The history of the DA cannot, of course, be separated from the covert career of its only chief, Manuel Piñeiro Losada (*Barba Roja*, or "Red Beard"), whose publicly reported activities also are documented herein (see Appendix 2 for biography).

II. THE GUEVARIST YEARS

Fidel Castro did not wait until taking power to launch his terrorist war against the U.S. presence in Latin America. After Castro's Department of Rebel Intelligence learned in late May 1958 that two of dictator Fulgencio Batista's airplanes had been loaded with U.S. arms and ammunition at the U.S. Naval Base at Guantánamo, the Castro brothers began planning a major terrorist operation against Americans in Cuba. That summer, 26th of July Movement (M-26) terrorists under Raúl Castro's command kidnapped fifty-seven North Americans, including a busload of twenty-seven U.S. sailors and Marines, and two Canadians.[10] The ensuing international hostage crisis threat-

---

[9] U.S. Departments of State and Defense, *The Soviet-Cuban Connection in Central America and the Caribbean*, March 1985, p. 10.

[10] Hugh Thomas, *The Cuban Revolution* (New York: Harper & Row Publishers, 1977), pp. 218-219.

ened to result in U.S. military action against the M-26, an event that could have thwarted Castro's seizure of power. Although the United States refused to meet Raúl Castro's ransom demands, which included ceasing all U.S. military support of the Batista regime, the Castro brothers gained worldwide publicity in releasing the hostages.

In 1959-60, within months after taking power, Castro and his chief of clandestine operations, Major "Ché" Guevara, undertook to export the Cuban revolutionary model by launching armed expeditions against Panama, Haiti, the Dominican Republic, and Nicaragua, but these exuberant attempts ended in total failure. In the case of Nicaragua, Eloy Gutiérrez Menoyo, a Cuban revolutionary hero who spent twenty-two years in Castro's prisons, revealed that he met clandestinely in Nicaragua with nascent forces building against General Anastasio Somoza Debayle in 1959. According to Gutiérrez, Castro and other senior leaders actually rejected helping the Nicaraguans who composed the anti-Somoza resistance because they were mostly centrists.[11] Instead, in 1961, the Cubans formed a Marxist-Leninist, anti-Somoza guerrilla organization that became known as the Sandinista National Liberation Front (FSLN). According to the brother of the late Carlos Fonseca Amador (the FSLN's Stalinist Nicaraguan founder), the Cuban ambassador in Nicaragua, Quintín Piño Machado, formed the FSLN; the Cubans then built it up and chose its leadership.[12]

Castro and Guevara also decided on a more systematic approach to exporting revolution by organizing guerrilla training programs in Cuba and, in late 1961, establishing the General Directorate of Intelligence (DGI) under the Ministry of the Interior (MININT). Castro named his MININT vice and technical minister, Major Manuel Piñeiro Losada, to the post of DGI chief. To provide a guerrilla support mechanism, Piñeiro and Guevara formed, under the DGI, three Liberation Committees—organized regionally for the Caribbean, Central America, and South America—that became known as the Liberation

---

[11] See Edward Schumacher, "Castro Said To Have Shunned '59 Anti-Samoza Bid," *New York Times,* December 28, 1986, p. 13, citing a news conference given by Gutiérrez.

[12] Georgie Anne Geyer, "Clearly Visible Origins," *Washington Times,* December 17, 1987, citing her interview with Fausto Amador.

Directorate (DL) (see Figure 1).[13] In the early 1960s, the DL also was responsible for supporting "liberation movements" in Africa. It trained and funded African revolutionaries, including those who overthrew the government of Zanzibar in 1963.[14] Whereas Guevara's revolutionary interests focused on Africa in the early 1960s, Piñeiro was more oriented toward the Western Hemisphere.

Figure 1: Evolution of the DA

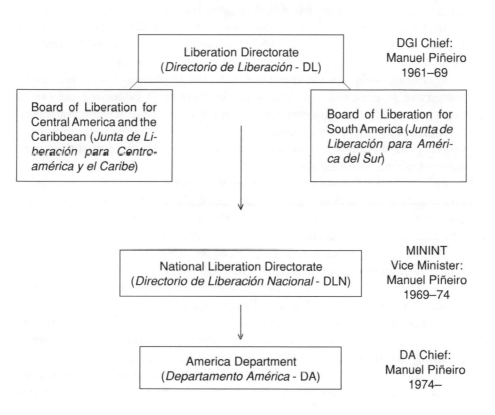

[13] See the OAS security report of 1962 in U.S. Congress, House, Committee on Foreign Affairs, *Castro-Communist Subversion in the Western Hemisphere*, 88th Cong., 2d sess., 1963, Appendix I, p. 272.

[14] Brian Crozier, "Soviet Pressures in the Caribbean: The Satellisation of Cuba," *Conflict Studies*, no. 35 (May 1973).

Evidence that DGI chief Piñeiro was directing guerrilla groups in Latin America in the early 1960s surfaced when the Colombian Army found a letter written by him to a group of Colombian rebels, whom he told to carry out Cuban instructions exactly as stated or else their monthly payment would be reduced or suspended.[15] On January 31, 1962, the Organization of American States (OAS) expelled Cuba for supporting Venezuelan guerrillas. Four days later, on February 4, a far from contrite Castro proclaimed his Second Declaration of Havana, in which he called on "the people" of the continent to "follow Cuba's example" by initiating guerrilla warfare.[16]

In an exchange of letters with Soviet Premier Nikita Khrushchev during the Cuban missile crisis of October 1962, President John F. Kennedy pledged that the United States would not invade Cuba if the Soviets withdrew all offensive strategic weapons and if Cuba agreed not to extend "its aggressive or subversive activities to any part of the hemisphere." Following the crisis, however, the Castro regime embarked on a policy of full support for armed revolution in Latin America. In a televised January 16, 1963, speech, Castro virtually declared war against the hemisphere, telling viewers that their duty was to lead the continent in Cuba-style revolution.

As a result of the OAS sanctions imposed on Cuba in July 1964 for its continued support of Venezuelan guerrillas, Cuban dependence on the Soviets increased. A compromise agreement that was worked out between Castro and the Latin American communist parties (CPs) that November lasted only until the U.S. intervention in the Dominican Republic in April 1965. The CPs, with Soviet approval, revoked their agreements to support guerrilla warfare in six countries and retreated to a less provocative "united front" strategy. Castro, however, decided to globalize Cuba's revolutionary role.

By hosting a series of international conferences of extremists in Havana during 1966-68, Castro succeeded in creating a nascent world terrorist fraternity and in strengthening his leadership role in it, especially in the Latin American movement. At the Tricontinental Conference, held in January 1966 and attended by 513 predominantly Castroite leaders of eighty-three Third

---

[15] The letter, published in Bogotá newspapers on October 17, 1963, is noted by Paul D. Bethel, *The Losers* (New Rochelle, N.Y.: Arlington House, 1969), p. 424.

[16] Andres Suárez, *Cuba: Castroism and Communism, 1959-1966* (Cambridge, Mass.: MIT Press, 1967), pp. 143-146.

World radical movements and CPs, Castro promised the delegates that "any revolutionary movement anywhere in the world can count on Cuba's unconditional support."[17] Nevertheless, Cuban support was no longer entirely unconditional. As Maurice Halperin points out, it was now contingent on recognition of: (1) Cuba's present and future military role in Latin American guerrilla operations, and (2) undisputed Cuban political leadership and direction of Latin American revolutionary movements.[18]

Castro clearly upstaged the Soviets at the Tricontinental Conference, but he partly appeased them by using the occasion to break with China and denounce and exclude the Trotskyites. He also ensured that the series of "armed struggle" resolutions that were adopted by the conference targeted mainly Colombia, Guatemala, Peru, and Venezuela—countries without major diplomatic or trade importance for the Soviets (who declined, however, to endorse "armed struggle" in Peru).[19] By the end of 1966, Cuba had established more than a dozen international guerrilla training camps under the supervision of Soviet KGB Colonels Vadim Kochergin and Viktor Simonov.[20] One of Colonel Simonov's first graduates was Ilich Ramírez Sánchez (a.k.a. "Carlos the Jackal").[21]

The Soviets and Cubans remained far apart on revolutionary strategy, however. The Soviets called for unifying revolutionary forces in a broad popular front, but Castro endorsed Guevara's grandiose scheme of creating "two, three, or many Vietnams" in the Western Hemisphere. Guevara dropped out of sight in March 1965 and fought covertly, along with about 300 Cubans,

---

[17] See U.S. Congress, Senate, Committee on the Judiciary, Internal Security Subcommittee, *The Tricontinental Conference of African, Asian, and Latin American Peoples*, 1966.

[18] Maurice Halperin, *The Taming of Fidel Castro* (Berkeley: University of California Press, 1981), p. 189.

[19] Senate, *Tricontinental*, p. 84.

[20] Christopher Dobson and Ronald Payne, *The Carlos Complex* (London: Coronet Books, 1977), p. 36; and Claire Sterling, *The Terror Network: The Secret War of International Terrorism* (New York: Holt, Rinehart & Winston, 1981), p. 15.

[21] Dobson and Payne, *Ibid.*, p. 36.

in Zaire (then called the Belgian Congo) for the next 12 months or so.[22]

After Guevara returned secretly to Cuba, Castro accepted his rationale for targeting Bolivia to be the *foco* (insurrectional center) of "continental revolution." Guevara thereupon infiltrated into Bolivia to organize a guerrilla campaign. DGI official Luís Fernández de Oña coordinated the Bolivian operation from DGI headquarters in Havana.[23] According to DGI defector Orlando Castro Hidalgo, Cuba actually "planned a two-pronged attack on South America," with the first prong emanating from Bolivia and the second from Venezuela.[24]

Soviet-Cuban relations deteriorated further as a result of the uncompromising "armed struggle"-line adopted at the meeting of the Latin American Solidarity Organization in Havana in the summer of 1967 and Castro's continued self-promotion. Nevertheless, adopted at the meeting was the important organizational principle of a "unified politico-military command." This action marked the beginning of a gradual shift in Castro's policy away from ineffectual Guevarism toward closer alignment with the more orthodox Marxist-Leninist strategy. The latter made Cuban support contingent not only on the existence of revolutionary conditions in a given country, but also on unification of the local guerrilla groups and Moscow-line CP. Guevara's death in combat in Bolivia in October 1967 effectively ended the era of *foco* theory, which was predicated on the unrealistic assumption that prior revolutionary conditions are not needed in order to foment a guerrilla insurgency.

III. SOVIET-CUBAN RAPPROCHEMENT

Soviet economic pressure on Cuba in 1967-68, including an oil embargo, forced Castro to finally capitulate to Soviet demands. These included adoption of a pro-Soviet/pro-CP line; cooperation in a two-pronged Soviet strategy of improving trade and diplomatic relations in Latin America while developing a more sophisticated and selective revolutionary strategy; and subordination

---

[22] "'Ché' Guevara fought in Africa, Cuban colonel says," French Press Agency, *Washington Times*, October 6, 1987, p. A9.

[23] Robert Moss, *Chile's Marxist Experiment* (Newton Abbot: David & Charles, 1973), p. 111.

[24] Orlando Castro Hidalgo, *Spy for Fidel* (Miami: E.A. Seemann Publishing, Inc., 1971), pp. 48-49.

of the DGI to the KGB.[25]

After taking control of the DGI, the KGB compelled Castro to replace its chief, Manuel Piñeiro, with José Méndez Cominches in 1969.[26] One theory posited that the Soviets had not forgiven Piñeiro, a Castro loyalist, for thwarting a KGB plot—in collusion with a pro-Soviet "microfaction" of the PCC/CC—to oust Castro in early 1968 and replace him with a party member more amenable to Moscow's orders.[27] Nevertheless, Castro kept Piñeiro in his other position as MININT vice minister, and also gave him supervisory control over the 400-member DL staff.

Gerardo Peraza, a former DGI official who defected in 1971, affirmed that the Soviets had "allowed Castro to take Manuel Piñeiro away and name him head of the Department of Liberation, and the intelligence service remained under the orders of Colonel Simonov."[28] Peraza added that the Soviets tried to "bolster Fidel Castro's ego" by giving him "the power or the freedom to work against the Latin American countries, such as Nicaragua, El Salvador."[29] Castro Hidalgo described the terms of the agreement as follows:

> Castro will faithfully follow Soviet policy when basic Soviet interests are involved. Where basic Soviet diplomatic and commercial interests are not involved, the Cuban government will be permitted to undertake revolutionary adventures.[30]

---

[25] John Barron, *KGB: The Secret Work of Soviet Secret Agents* (New York: Bantam Books, 1974), p. 205; and U.S. Congress, Senate, Committee on the Judiciary, Internal Security Subcommittee, Hearings, Part 20, *Communist Threat to the United States Through the Caribbean*, October 16, 1969, p. 1425, citing the testimony of DGI defector Orlando Castro Hidalgo.

[26] Barron, *KGB*, p. 206.

[27] Barron, *KGB*, pp. 203-204; also see U.S. Senate investigator Alfonso L. Tarabochia's testimony in U.S. Congress, Senate, Committee on the Judiciary, Internal Security Subcommittee, *Terroristic Activity: The Castro Connection in Puerto Rico: Castro's Hand in Puerto Rican and U.S. Terrorism*, 94th Cong., 1st sess., Part 6, July 30, 1975, p. 379.

[28] U.S. Congress, Senate, Committee on the Judiciary, *The Role of Cuba in International Terrorism and Subversion*, 97th Cong., 2d sess., 1982, p. 9.

[29] *Ibid.*

[30] Senate, *Communist Threat*, p. 1426.

The organization that Castro created in 1969 to oversee these adventures was the National Liberation Directorate (DLN), which was soon made independent of the MININT.[31] Thus, the DL became the DLN, with Piñeiro as its chief. Meanwhile, according to Peraza, the DGI reorganized, "adopting the same structure of the intelligence service in the Soviet Union," in order to provide the Soviets with the intelligence on the United States that they now required of the DGI.[32] This included creating separate departments for Economic and Military Intelligence against the United States, Political Information, and Foreign Counterintelligence.[33] Whereas the activities of the DGI and DL/DLN previously had overlapped considerably, these agencies now operated under a greater division of labor.

For example, Peraza explained that until the DGI's reorganization in 1970, both the DGI and DL had operated jointly against Puerto Rico. Henceforth, the DGI would focus its efforts on collecting military, political, and economic information about the United States (i.e., espionage) and would no longer be involved in supporting Puerto Rican terrorists; the DLN would assume that duty.[34] Peraza also noted that, subsequent to 1970, the DGI could "count on any means" of Soviet support, whereas "the Department of Liberation of Latin America and Africa has a limited amount of money and a limited quantity of weapons and other means."[35] In other words, the Soviets allowed Castro to keep Piñeiro, but the agency that he headed lacked bureaucratic status.

The DLN's emergence coincided with a significant change in Cuban revolutionary strategy and tactics. As Castro Hidalgo explained, the Cubans decided not to send any more Cuban military leaders to assist guerrilla groups until a significant level of revolutionary development was reached and the Cubans were invited in by the guerrilla leaders.[36] Guevara's fiasco in Bolivia had convinced the Cubans of the impracticality of having Cuban-led and Cuban-manned guerrilla groups in another Latin country, because of nation-

---

[31] D.L. West, "Cuba III," *Tecnología Militar* [Bonn] 3 (1983), pp. 145-146.

[32] Peraza testimony, *op cit*, p. 7.

[33] *Ibid.*

[34] Peraza, p. 12.

[35] *Ibid.*, p. 9.

[36] Senate, *Communist Threat*, p. 1426.

alistic and cultural sensitivities of the local rebel and CP groups. The DLN's limited budget also appeared to have dictated this change of tactics.

During the 1970-73 period, Castro complied with the Soviet broad-front strategy in Latin America by pursuing a policy of ostensibly normalizing relations with numerous Latin American countries. The rural guerrilla groups that Cuba had supported in the 1960s remained inactive either because they no longer qualified for material Cuban aid or Cuba lacked the resources to support them in any case. Nevertheless, the Castro regime did maintain ties to those groups, providing them with safe-haven, training, and propaganda support.[37] Urban terrorist groups, such as the National Liberation Movement (MLN)/ Tupamaros of Uruguay, also received low-key Cuban support. After the MLN's defeat in 1972, several hundred members fled to Cuba, where many then underwent extensive training in military and terrorist tactics, weapons familiarity, and intelligence methods.[38] The Argentinean Montoneros and People's Revolutionary Army (ERP) also received tactical and organizational advice and training in urban and rural guerrilla techniques in Cuba.[39]

During the 1970-73 period of Salvador Allende's Socialist regime in Chile, the DLN also trained many members of the Movement of the Revolutionary Left (MIR), reportedly with North Korean help. The Cubans supplied the radical left in Chile with large quantities of Soviet- and Czechoslovakian-made weapons delivered by Cubana Airlines and Cuban merchant ships.[40] As in Buenos Aires, the Cuban embassy in Santiago was actively involved in subversive activities, but on a much larger scale. From their coordinating center in Santiago, the Cubans maintained liaison with "liberation movements" in Argentina, Bolivia, and Uruguay.[41] According to Robert Moss, about three-quarters of the 150-member Cuban embassy staff "were thought

---

[37] U.S. Department of State, Bureau of Public Affairs, *Cuba's Renewed Support For Violence in Latin America*, Special Report No. 90, December 14, 1981, p. 12.

[38] Sterling, *Terror Network*, p. 11.

[39] State Dept., *Cuba's Renewed Support*, p. 11.

[40] *Ibid.*

[41] James Theberge, "Kremlin's Hand in Chile," *Soviet Analyst*, August 15, 1974, as reprinted in U.S. Congress, House, Committee on Foreign Affairs, *United States and Chile During the Allende Years, 1970-73*, 1975, p. 636.

to be involved in intelligence work."[42] The Cuban support apparatus apparently extended to *La Moneda*, the presidential palace. Moss reported that Cuban operative Fernández de Oña worked in *La Moneda* and that a senior DGI officer directly supervised Allende's foreign communications.[43] Fernández had married Allende's daughter Beatriz, who later was reported to have committed suicide in Havana.[44]

As anti-Allende opposition increased during 1973, Castro sent a handwritten letter to Allende, dated July 29, 1973, informing him that he was sending DLN chief Piñeiro to Chile under false pretenses for the purpose of evaluating the situation and offering expert advice.[45] After his arrival in Santiago on July 30, accompanied by Vice Prime Minister Carlos Rafael Rodríguez, Piñeiro personally delivered this letter to Allende. According to former U.S. Ambassador Nathaniel Davis, Piñeiro and Rodríguez were widely suspected of coming to advise the government on ways to deal with the mounting political and military opposition.[46] The two Cuban officials left after five days, having made private recommendations to Allende. The subsequent firing of two generals was believed to be one of the recommended measures.[47] After the military coup and Allende's death, Castro promised Chilean radicals "all the aid in Cuba's power to provide."

Allende's overthrow thoroughly discredited the Soviet "peaceful road" in Latin America, and vindicated Castro's "armed struggle" doctrine. Boris Ponomarev, the CPSU's International Department chief, affirmed in a post mortem that Communists must be prepared "to reply with revolutionary violence to the reactionary violence of the bourgeoisie."[48] His reassessment

---

[42] Moss, *op cit*, p. 111.

[43] *Ibid.*

[44] Fernández was last reported in 1976 as chief of an unidentified DA Section. CIA, *Directory*, November 1985, p. 8.

[45] For a copy of the letter, see OAS, Special Consultative Commission on Security, *The Marxist-Leninist Process in Chile*, 1974, pp. 233-234.

[46] Nathaniel Davis, *The Last Two Years of Salvador Allende* (Ithaca, New York: Cornell University Press, 1985), pp. 184-185.

[47] *Ibid.*

[48] As cited by León Gouré and Morris Rothenberg, *Soviet Penetration of Latin America* (Coral Gables: University of Miami Press, 1975), p. 111.

indicated that the Brezhnev regime had abandoned the Khrushchev doctrine of "peaceful transition to socialism" in the Third World in favor of a political-military strategy. Robert Leiken points out that "Soviet tactics underwent major innovations" during this period, such as the official declaration that "political-military fronts" modeled on Castro's former M-26 could play the vanguard role previously accorded the CPs.[49]

The creation of the Revolutionary Coordinating Junta (JCR) in Buenos Aires in February 1974 inaugurated the launching of the Cuban-Soviet political-military revolutionary strategy in the Southern Cone. Although the JCR ostensibly was founded as an umbrella coordinating organization by four South American groups—the Bolivian National Liberation Army (ELN), the Argentinean ERP, the Chilean MIR, and the Uruguayan MLN—the DGI was reportedly the organizing force behind it.[50] In the early 1970s, the Cuban embassy in Buenos Aires served as a direct liaison with the Montoneros and ERP.[51] DA official Roberto Cabrera, then a presumed DLN operative, began serving as first secretary of the Cuban embassy in Buenos Aires in mid-1973.[52] (Cabrera reportedly still held that position in August 1983, in addition to serving as chief of an unidentified South American Section of the DA.[53] According to Jay Mallin, however, DA official Damián Arteaga Hernández was serving as first secretary in Buenos Aires in 1983.[54])

Prospects for "armed struggle" in the Southern Cone appeared bleak with the military coup in Argentina in 1976 and the subsequent decimation of the ERP. After police raided the elaborate underground JCR headquarters outside Buenos Aires in 1977, it was moved to Paris.[55] By 1978, the Montoneros also had been defeated and Cuba allowed its national leadership to headquarter in

---

[49] Robert S. Leiken, "Fantasies and Facts: The Soviet Union and Nicaragua," *Current History* (October 1984), p. 315.

[50] For example, see Everett G. Martin, "Latin America's Terrorist Network," *Wall Street Journal* , April 15, 1980, p. 24.

[51] State Dept., *Cuba's Renewed Support*, p. 12.

[52] CIA, *Directory*, November 1985.

[53] *Ibid.*, pp. 8, 221.

[54] Mallin, "Cuban Intelligence Elite," *op cit.*

[55] Sterling, *Terror Network*, p. 110.

Havana.[56] In Paris and other West European cities, the JCR network reportedly operated in conjunction with the DGI, running a covert documentation center for forged passports and identity cards, carrying out fund-raising kidnapping, propagandizing, and maintaining contact with training camps for Latin Americans in Cuba.[57] The principal JCR training camp in Cuba was, and reportedly has remained, a 4,000-acre estate near Guanabo, staffed by Cuban officers.[58]

At a meeting of Latin American CPs in Havana in June 1975, Castro, as PCC First Secretary, received a formal mandate to unify, coordinate, and support CPs and other Marxist-Leninist groups and to promote "armed struggle" in numerous Latin American countries.[59] Castro's only real concessions were to agree to be more selective about supporting guerrilla groups and to cooperate with the local CP in each of the countries where this strategy would be pursued. This policy was in Castro's own interest because by 1975 he had re-established relations with ten OAS-member states, and the OAS lifted diplomatic sanctions on Cuba that July.

The myth that Castro had abandoned "armed struggle" in Latin America in favor of a good neighbor policy is further belied by Article 12(c) of the Castro regime's first Socialist Constitution, promulgated in February 1976. It states that Cuba "recognizes the legitimacy of the wars of national liberation." It also codifies Ponomarev's tenet: "the right of peoples to repel imperialist and reactionary violence with revolutionary violence."[60] (Article 28 of the new Soviet Constitution, adopted in 1977, likewise supports "national liberation" struggles.)

Following his successful airlifting of Cuban troops to Angola in the mid-1970s to ensure a Marxist seizure of power, Castro visited Moscow in early

---

[56] State Dept., *Cuba's Renewed Support*, p. 11.

[57] "Worldwide Terrorist Activities Are Planned and Financed by International HQ in Paris," *The Times* [London], October 18, 1977.

[58] Sterling, p. 110, citing *Economist Foreign Report*, March 23, 1977.

[59] For the text of the final communiqué, see William E. Ratliff, *Castroism and Communism in Latin America, 1959-1976* (Washington/Stanford: AEI-Hoover Policy Studies, 1976), Appendix D, pp. 217-232.

[60] For excerpts, see Lester A. Sobel, ed., *Castro's Cuba in the 1970s* (New York: Facts on File, 1978), pp. 169-170.

April 1977 and signed an agreement with the Soviets, who pledged further Communist support for guerrilla movements in Asia, Africa, and Latin America. A Soviet communiqué stated that Castro and Brezhnev had resolved to do everything they could "for promoting the international Communist national liberation movements...."[61] His prestige enhanced, Castro began focusing on revolutionary prospects in Central America, where human rights issues had come to the fore.

IV. THE PCC/CC's "GUERRILLA INTERNATIONAL"

In December 1974, Castro reorganized the independent DLN into the America Department (DA). It was placed under the PCC/CC in order to centralize Cuban operational control over covert activities required to implement the new revolutionary strategy.[62] Since then, the PCC/CC's covert action apparatus for supporting so-called "national liberation movements" and the subversive efforts of radical regimes in the hemisphere, namely Nicaragua and formerly Grenada, has been organized around the DA. This agency plans and coordinates most of Cuba's covert operations in support of the Cuban-Soviet revolutionary strategy in the Americas. DA activities include operating secret guerrilla and terrorist training camps in Cuba, networks for the covert movement of personnel and materiel between Cuba and targeted Latin American countries, and an extensive propaganda apparatus.[63] According to Mallin, DA agents also have operated in Europe and other regions in support of DA operations in the Americas.[64]

Singular only in name, the DA is in actuality a Department of the Americas. Piñeiro organized the DA into four regional sections—Central America, South America, the Caribbean, and North America—as well as a Center for Latin American Studies (CEAL), a Center for North American Studies (CEA), and seven unidentified sections (see Figure 2).[65] Covers often used by DA officials

---

[61] Christopher S. Wren, "Soviet Union and Cuba Promise More Aid for Guerrilla Groups," *New York Times*, April 9, 1977.

[62] State Dept., *Cuba's Renewed Support*, p. 4.

[63] *Ibid.*

[64] Mallin, "Cuban Intelligence elite," *op cit.*

[65] CIA, *Directory*, pp. 7-8.

Figure 2: Organization of the
PCC/CC's Revolutionary Affairs Apparatus

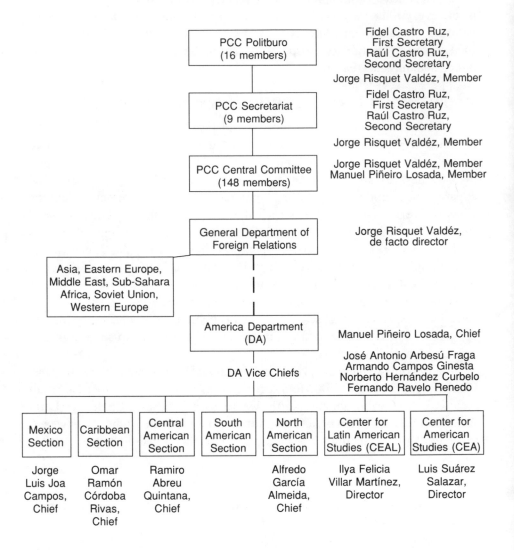

[Source: Data compiled largely from U.S. Central Intelligence Agency, *Directory of Officials of the Republic of Cuba*, op cit, 1987, pp. 7-8. The Directory lists an additional six chiefs of unidentified sections. The Directory inconsistently refers to DA vice chiefs as deputy chiefs, although it uses "vice" in referring to vice ministers.]

are as diplomats, employees of Cuba's Prensa Latina news agency, Cubana Airlines, the Institute for Friendship With the Peoples (ICAP), and Cuban-front companies.[66] Much of the activities of Cuba's extensive international media apparatus, cultural exchanges, and political indoctrination programs are known to be designed to support covert operations and to promote active solidarity with or support for "armed struggle" in Latin America.[67]

Castro's formation of the DA under the PCC/CC also reflected his desire to qualify for Soviet support of his revolutionary program. The former DLN reportedly had not received any support since its creation in 1969 because the Soviets preferred to channel their aid through the CPs rather than an independent Cuban agency not under their direct control. The lack of Soviet support helps to explain Castro's limited aid to guerrilla groups during the 1969-73 period. Moreover, the DLN reportedly lost influence in Cuban foreign affairs, whereas the Soviet-controlled DGI and PCC gained it. Predictably, Castro persuaded the Soviets to allow him to name Piñeiro as head of the DA. "Red Beard" thereupon emerged from his relative obscurity as DLN chief since 1969.

Although usually overlooked by most U.S. analysts who analyze Cuba's revolutionary activities in the hemisphere, the DA, as described by Jay Mallin—one of the few correspondents, perhaps the only one, to have reported on the agency in any detail—"is one of the smallest, most dangerous and least known" of the major intelligence agencies of the world.[68] Mallin reported in 1983 that the DA had between 200 and 300 members.[69] The DA is dangerous not only because it supports and guides terrorist organizations, but also because it is effective, as demonstrated by its successful operation in support of the FSLN in 1978-79. The Nicaraguan resistance appeared to be on the verge of abandoning its anti-Sandinista war in the fall of 1988, while the Farabundo Martí National Liberation Front (FMLN) in El Salvador was

---

[66] State Dept., *Cuba's Renewed Support*, p. 4.

[67] *Ibid.*

[68] Jay Mallin, "How Cuban Agents Deliver Arms to Leftist Guerrillas in El Salvador," *Washington Times*, August 22, 1983, p. A1.

[69] Jay Mallin, "Cuban Intelligence Elite Pushes Subversion in the Americas," *Washington Times*, August 25, 1983, p. 7A.

stepping up its "armed struggle," thanks in part to the effectiveness of DA-conducted lobbying/propaganda campaigns.

The DA draws on the expertise and support of the DGI.[70] According to *The Economist*, "There is no hard-and-fast division of labour..." between the DA and DGI; "they will share their manpower to conduct specific operations, and many career intelligence officers are transferred back and forth from the DGI to the [America Department]."[71] Although the extent of this reported DA-DGI interaction is not clear, there appears to be a greater division of labor than *The Economist* report suggests. For example, one high-level Nicaraguan government security defector, Miguel Bolaños Hunter, revealed that the DA is the "most powerful" branch of the Cuban security apparatus. According to Bolaños, DA personnel regard themselves as the elite of the various Cuban security agencies, and the DA is accorded more respect and prestige in Cuba, as well as among the Soviets.[72]

DGI support may include providing some funds. According to Major Florentino Aspillaga Lombard, a former high-ranking MININT security official who defected to the United States in June 1987, each year MININT agents stationed abroad customarily bestow Fidel Castro with millions of Cuban *pesos* on the occasion of his birthday on August 13. Castro received 3.7-million Cuban *pesos* in 1985 and 4.2-million in 1986. These monies, generated as a result of illicit businesses, are never deposited in the National Bank of Cuba. Instead, Castro usually deposits them, presumably not as *pesos*, in a Swiss bank and spends them to support favored guerrilla movements or bribe leaders.[73] Aspillaga complained that Piñeiro's DA had spent "millions and millions" of dollars trying to make revolution in Latin America, without any

---

[70] State Department, *Cuba's Renewed Support*, p. 4.

[71] "Special Report on Cuba," *Foreign Report*, November 7, 1979, p. 2.

[72] See the exerpts from an interview with Bolaños in Uri Ra'anan, Robert L. Pfaltzgraff, *et alia*, eds., *Hydra of Carnage* (Lexington, Mass.: Lexington Books, 1986), p. 315.

[73] United States Information Agency, Radio Martí Program, "The Defection of A MININT Official," *Cuba—Quarterly Situation Report, Third Quarter 1987*, p. V-13. Also see Radio Martí Program's Interview with Aspillaga, August 1987, Tape 1, Side 2, p. 4.

positive result because the peoples have opposed these efforts.[74] Aspillaga added that DA officials live like kings in Cuba, especially Piñeiro, who has spent "enormous" sums of money "trying to live well." Carlos Franqui noted that Piñeiro was living like a baron even in the early 1960s.[75]

The DA's Regional Studies Centers: Two of the fronts used by the DA— CEA and CEAL—also have been useful in masking the DA's activities in diplomatic and academic circles. The CEA is part of the DA's North American Section, which in 1986 was headed by Alfredo García Almeida, a former member of the Cuban Interests Section in Washington, D.C.[76] In an article published in early 1988, Jorge Domínguez described the PCC/CC's CEA as a "new think tank" composed of "Cuban scholars."[77] His description is misleading in several respects. The CEA, which was headed in 1986 by DA official Luis Suárez Salazar,[78] is a "think tank" only in the sense that a few of its members present propagandistic papers at theoretical or academic conferences, and others study ways to exploit U.S. security vulnerabilities. In mid-1983, the CEA published, in Havana, the first issue of the biannual *Cuadernos de Nuestra America (Record of Our America)*, containing articles on such topics as "Annexationist Trends in the Puerto Rican Political Process" and "Economic Interests Involved in Military Production in the United States."

In recent years, CEA "scholars" have been invited to conferences of the Latin American Studies Association (LASA), but were unable to obtain visas until LASA's meeting in New Orleans in March 1988. At this conference, the CEA sponsored a panel entitled "Cuba and Central America in U.S. Foreign Policy." Organized by CEA official Juan Valdés Paz, the panel's presenters included him and two other CEA "scholars": Julio Carranza Valdés and Rafael Hernández. Valdés' paper dealt with "U.S. Strategic Foreign Policy in Central

---

[74] Bill Gertz, "Defector Charges Castro Poking Nose in U.S. Race," *Washington Times*, March 25, 1988, p.A3.

[75] Carlos Franqui, *Diary of the Cuban Revolution* (New York: Viking Press, 1980).

[76] CIA, *Directory*, 1987, p.7; Mallin, "Elite," *op cit.*

[77] Jorge I. Domínguez, "Cuba in the International Arena," *Latin American Research Review*, v. 23, no. 1 (1988), p. 202.

[78] CIA, *Directory*, June 1987, p. 8.

America." Manuel Díaz, First Secretary of the Cuban Interests Section, also appeared at a number of the meetings on U.S.-Cuban relations.[79]

The non-academic activities of CEA and CEAL officials indicate that they are actually Communist bloc intelligence operatives. CEA and CEAL officials play key roles in coordinating terrorist and other subversive activities in support of Marxist-Leninist groups throughout the hemisphere. For example, the Cuban Chargé d'Affaires in Nicaragua in the early 1980s was Luís Hernández Ojeda, a member of the DA's CEAL.[80] In the late 1970s, Hernández coordinated FSLN operations from Panama. Another CEAL official, Fernando Comas, also coordinated FSLN operations and later played an important role in unifying Puerto Rican terrorist groups.

The DGRE: The PCC/CC's General Department of Foreign Relations (DGRE) is the Cuban counterpart of the CPSU's International Department and the Department for Liaison with Communist and Workers' Parties of Socialist Countries. As such, the DGRE is the Cuban agency responsible for covert revolutionary activities and overt diplomatic relations with extremist groups, Communist parties, and radical political parties and regimes worldwide. Its regional responsibilities are Asia, Eastern Europe, Middle East, Sub-Sahara Africa, the Soviet Union, and Western Europe (see Figure 2).[81] From 1979 to at least April 1987, Jesús Montané Oropesa, then an alternate member of the Politburo and a member of the Secretariat, headed the DGRE. Although said to be one of Fidel Castro's closest associates, Montané had a reputation as a hard-liner who was closer to Raúl Castro.[82] By mid-1987, Montané apparently had been replaced by a much higher-ranking official, Jorge Risquet Valdés, a

---

[79] Alfred Padula, "Cuba, as Always, Sparks Much Interest at LASA," *The Times of the Americas*, April 6, 1988, p.5.

[80] CIA, *Directory*, pp. 9, 235.

[81] CIA, *Directory*, June 1987, pp. 10-11.

[82] On Montané, see: Herbert L. Matthews, *Fidel Castro* (New York: Simon & Shuster, 1970), pp. 65-5, 73; Matthews, *Revolution in Cuba* (New York: Charles Scribner's Sons, 1975), pp. 16, 51, 53, 253; Hugh Thomas, *The Cuban Revolution* (New York: Harper & Row Publishers, 1971), pp. 39, 91; K.S. Karol, *Guerrillas in Power* (New York: Hill & Wang, 1970), p. 311; John Dorschner and Robert Fabricio, *The Winds of December* (New York: Coward, McCann and Geoghegan, 1980), pp. 170, 445; and Franqui, *Diary*, pp. 49-55, 528.

member of the PCC's Politburo and Secretariat.[83] Montané was also dropped from his PCC posts, but remained a PCC/CC member and reportedly a close Castro adviser, responsible mainly for coordinating Central American and Caribbean CPs. For example, Montané coordinated a "consultative meeting of Caribbean anti-imperialist organizations" on June 11-13, 1984, and headed the Cuban delegation to the so-called First Central American and Caribbean Solidarity Meeting with Panama on March 29, 1988.[84]

Organizationally, the DA appears to be the DGRE's semi-autonomous hemispheric division (see Figure 2). The DGRE carries out functions similar to those of the DA, but in different regions of the world. Although observers generally agree that Piñeiro answers directly to Fidel Castro, the two agencies—DA and DGRE—apparently work together to some extent in conducting relations with foreign groups and governments under their respective purviews, as well as carrying out support operations. For example, the DA and DGRE have funneled a variety of untraceable small arms and ammunition to guerrilla groups through an international network of 130 Cuban-owned front companies operating in eleven Latin American and three African countries, as well as Canada, Japan, and much of Western Europe.[85] There is also probably some personnel interaction between the two agencies. One official, Germán Sánchez, was reported in 1983 as chief of unidentified sections in both the DGRE and DA, but in 1986 he was with the DGRE only.[86]

V. THE NICARAGUAN REVOLUTIONARY MODEL

After the FSLN's Third Line guerrilla faction opened an impressive countrywide offensive against the Somoza regime in October 1977, Castro decided to make Nicaragua the DA's first Central American target. Manuel Piñeiro's deputy, Armando Estrada Fernández, began making numerous

---

[83] USIA, Radio Martí Program, *Cuba—Quarterly Situation Report: First Quarter 1987*, p. VI-9.

[84] *Granma,* March 30, 1988, p. 8; and *FBIS,* vol. 6, June 13, 1984, citing Havana Domestic Service.

[85] Roger Fontaine, "Cuba-backed Fronts Evade U.S. Embargo," *Washington Times*, May 23, 1986, p. 1A; Roger Fontaine and James Morrison, "Defector Brings Insider's View From Havana," *Washington Times*, July 29, 1986.

[86] CIA, *Directory*, June 1984, pp. 8, 13; and June 1987, p. 11.

clandestine trips to the region to both promote the unification of the three FSLN factions and lay the groundwork for an arms supply network.[87] Estrada was a former chief of the DGI's Middle East and Africa sections, with experience in training Palestinian guerrillas.[88] The Cubans also began training FSLN guerrilla forces in Cuba. The KGB is believed to have assisted the Cuban efforts to train, fund, and arm the FSLN.[89]

In September 1978, Cuban arms, other supplies, and Cuban-trained FSLN members arrived at staging sites in northern Costa Rica via small aircraft flown from Panama, and later in Panamanian Air Force planes.[90] Cuban news media reported the arrival in Havana of the FSLN's senior leader, Tomás Borge, on September 26, his reception by Estrada, and his meeting with Castro on the 27th. By the end of the year, arms began arriving in Costa Rica directly from Cuba. Accompanying them were members of the elite Special Troops (*Spetsnaz*) from the MININT's Directorate of Special Operations (DOE) to oversee the equipping of the rebels and to help coordinate guerrilla operations.[91] On December 26, the Cubans announced the decision of the FSLN factions to merge.

In early 1979, DA agents helped to organize, arm, and transport an International Brigade to fight with the FSLN. A senior DA guerrilla warfare specialist, Pedro González Piñeiro (Commander "Justo"), served as the field adviser to the brigade.[92] By that April, the FSLN factional leaders had formed a unified FSLN National Directorate as a result of a series of talks in Havana with Fidel Castro and DA officials.[93]

When Carlos Andrés Pérez's tenure as President of Venezuela ended that

---

[87] State Dept., *Cuba's Renewed Support*, p.5.

[88] Castro Hidalgo, p. 106.

[89] Jiri and Virginia Valenta, "Sandinistas in Power." *Problems of Communism*, September-October 1985, p. 5. FSLN veterans are also known to have received training at PLO camps in Lebanon and Libya beginning in the early 1970s. See U.S. Department of State, *The Sandinistas and Middle Eastern Radicals*, August 1985, pp. 1-2, 6.

[90] State Dept., *Cuba's Renewed Support*, p. 6.

[91] *Ibid.*

[92] "Special Report," *Foreign Report*, p. 7.

[93] State Dept., *Cuba's Renewed Support*, p. 5; and *Granma*, March 28, 1979.

spring, the FSLN's principal foreign source of logistical support dried up.[94] Consequently, Cuba became the FSLN's main supplier of military materiel and other essential support.[95] This change of foreign patron states usually has been ignored by those who view Cuba's role in the Nicaraguan revolution as insignificant. During the 1978-79 period, there were at least twenty-one flights between Cuba and Costa Rica carrying war materiel for the FSLN; a minimum of 500 tons of arms destined for the Sandinista forces were airlifted to Costa Rica from Cuba and elsewhere.[96] According to Aspillaga, however, a total of fifty-seven flights were made between Havana and Costa Rica, for a total of 1.8-million tons (as stated) of arms; Piñeiro personally supervised the loading operations at Havana airport. Julián López Díaz, then chief of the DA's Central American Section, directed the Cubans' main operations center—based in San José, Costa Rica—for coordinating logistics and contacts with the FSLN and monitoring the airlift.[97] When the FSLN launched its final offensive in mid-1979, Special Troops from the MININT's DOE were with Sandinista columns and maintained direct radio communications with Havana.[98]

After Somoza's ouster by the Cuban-supported FSLN forces in July 1979, Nicaragua quickly became a base of operations for the Cubans, particularly the DA. By mid-1979, the DA—now working through Nicaragua—had begun to impose the victorious "Nicaraguan model" on Marxist-Leninist movements in El Salvador, Guatemala, the Caribbean, Colombia, and Chile.[99] Expanding on the aforementioned Cuban-Soviet model, Cuban aid was made conditional on the successful implementation of a strategy of prolonged guerrilla warfare combining ultimately with urban insurrection and supported politically by a broad front of non-Communist opposition groups. Despite the contentions

---

[94] U.S. Departments of State and Defense, *Background Paper: Nicaragua's Military Build-Up and Support for Central American Subversion*, July 18, 1984, p. 12.

[95] *Ibid.*

[96] For the Costa Rican Special Legislative Commission Report see "Panamanian, Cuba Involvement in Arms Traffic Reported," *Latin America Report*, Joint Publications Research Service (JPRS), June 17, 1981, #78316, pp. 19-23.

[97] State Dept., *Cuba's Renewed Support*, p. 8.

[98] *Ibid.*

[99] See, for example, "Castro said trying to unify Central American guerrillas," *FBIS*, vol. 6, July 6, 1979, p. P3.

of those who minimize the Cuban-Soviet role, this model was not an endogenous Nicaraguan variety of revolution.[100]

Quietly taking credit for the revolution, the Soviets joined the Cubans in declaring the Nicaraguan model a "correct" revolutionary paradigm for other Central American nations. Z. Zagladin, deputy chief of the CPSU's International Department, linked the "victory of Nicaragua" to Soviet/Cuban-supported "anti-imperialist" strategy and expressed the hope that Nicaragua will have its "continuators."[101]

Following the FSLN's victory, the Soviets began to urge certain Latin American CPs to coordinate with guerrilla groups and agreed that "political-military fronts" should play the primary role in the creation of united fronts. Although the CP would remain the inheritor of revolution, it would concede the role of instigator to the "political-military front."[102] The CPs of Central America, Panama, and Mexico adopted the new Soviet line at a clandestine meeting held in October 1980.[103] (The Communist Party of El Salvador [PCES] already had decided by April 1979 to convert its entire party apparatus into a military-oriented organization.[104]) Nicaragua's ruling FSLN leaders have assisted the Cubans in playing an active role in promoting the Soviet policy of furthering cooperation between Latin American CPs and guerrilla groups.[105]

---

[100] For example, Ernest Evans, in his monograph "Revolutionary Movements in Central America: The Development of a New Strategy," in Howard J. Wiarda, ed. *Rift and Revolution: The Central American Imbroglio* (Washington: AEI, 1984), pp. 178-80, contends inaccurately that the "Sandinista model" was developed by the FSLN.

[101] As cited by Jiri Valenta, "The USSR, Cuba, and the crisis in Central America," *Orbis* 25 (31) (Fall 1981), p. 734.

[102] As cited by C.G. Jacobsen, "The Jacobsen Report: Soviet Attitudes Towards, and Contacts With, Central American Revolutionaries," U.S. Department of State External Research Program, April 10, 1984, p. 10.

[103] "Communist Parties Signal Major Changes," *Latin America Weekly Report* (London), December 12, 1980, pp. 9-10.

[104] Schafik Jorge Handal, "Power, the Character and Path of the Revolution and Unity of the Left," *Communist Affairs* [UK], no. 2 (1982), pp. 240-241.

[105] For example, FSLN and Cuban delegations attended the July 1984 meeting of South American CPs in Buenos Aires. See, "Statement By a Meeting of the Communist Parties of South America," *Information Bulletin* (Toronto), October 1984, p. 32.

In a paper presented to Latin American revolutionaries attending the International Theoretical Conference in Havana on April 27, 1982, DA chief Manuel Piñeiro reaffirmed the viability of the political-military model. He advocated the antithesis of the old Guevarist doctrine by arguing that "revolutionary strategy can be efficacious only to the extent that it adapts itself to the specific realities of each country" and "the strategic objectives of the revolution."[106] Because each revolutionary movement is different, Piñeiro reasoned, "only a political-military strategic conception and the corresponding training and preparation" will enable the guerrilla groups to implement the new revolutionary strategy effectively.[107] Piñeiro argued further that "the consistent and opportune use of arms" is an "important factor" that "combined with the unity of the masses...in our opinion guarantees the triumph of the genuine revolutionaries."[108]

VI. CASTRO'S NICARAGUAN "ROBOT"

Castro and Piñeiro have understandably been confident about their prospects for spreading subversion in Latin America in view of the remarkable success of the Cuban diplomatic stratagem in South America in disguising the true nature of Cuban activities in the region; the increasing Cubanization of Nicaragua; the conflict between the White House and Congress over support for the anti-Sandinista resistance; and the growing transnational guerrilla and terrorist cooperation in Latin America.

On August 30, 1984, Piñeiro cited four reasons for his optimism about revolutionary trends despite the Grenada setback: (1) the Cuban revolution was stronger than ever; (2) Somoza no longer ruled in Nicaragua; (3) the oligarchy cannot destroy the revolutionary movement in El Salvador; and (4) representative democracies in Latin America were rebelling against "imperialist domination."[109] Significantly, Piñeiro did not say that the Sandinistas rule in

---

[106] See Manuel Piñeiro Losada, "The Present Crisis of Imperialism and the Revolutionary Process in Latin America and the Caribbean," *Cuba Socialista* [Havana: PCC/CC], no. 4 (September- November 1982), pp. 15-53.

[107] *Ibid.*, p. 52.

[108] *Ibid.*, p. 50.

[109] As cited by Dr. Kenneth Skoug, Jr., Director of the Office of Cuban Affairs. See U.S. Department of State, Bureau of Public Affairs, *The United States and Cuba*, Current Policy No. 646, December 17, 1984, p. 3.

Nicaragua, only that Somoza no longer ruled. After all, the Cubans give the orders, or, more specifically, Fidel Castro. Aspillaga, who once served as a Cuban intelligence adviser to the Sandinista leaders, stated in August 1987 that, "The one who is controlling Nicaragua is Fidel, and that control today is total...."

An early indication of the central role that the DA would play in the Cuban-Nicaraguan relationship was Manuel Piñeiro's attendance at a meeting in Havana on July 27, 1979, at which diplomatic ties between the two countries were re-established after a quarter-century interruption.[110] On that occasion, DA official Julián López Díaz was named Ambassador to Nicaragua.[111] Piñeiro's prominent role in Cuba's relationship with the Sandinista regime in Nicaragua was underscored by his attendance at the first anniversary celebration of the FSLN-Cuban takeover, held in Managua in July 1980.[112] On that occasion, according to Robert Moss's sources, Castro, Piñeiro, and PCC Secretary General René Theodor held a secret meeting in Monimbó, Nicaragua, with Central American revolutionaries and Cuban agents from the United States. Castro reportedly boasted to the congregation that Cuba would spread revolution throughout Central America and develop the capacity to spark a race war in the United States.[113] In August 1980, Piñeiro reiterated Castro's plans at another secret meeting with terrorists held in Caracas, Venezuela.[114]

In January 1985, Fidel Castro, accompanied by Manuel Piñeiro, paid the Sandinista leaders an unannounced, surprise visit on the occasion of Daniel Ortega's investiture as president. Castro's action reflected the Cuban colonialist attitude in Nicaragua that Antonio Farach, a former Nicaraguan diplomat in Venezuela who defected in September 1983, commented on in testimony to Congress. Farach stated:

---

[110] "Diplomatic Relations Established with Nicaragua," *Latin America Report, FBIS*, vol. 6, July 30, 1979, p. Q1, citing Havana Radio.

[111] State Dept., *Cuba's Renewed Support*, p. 6.

[112] Robert Moss discusses the visit in U.S. Congress, Senate, Committee on the Judiciary, Subcommittee on Security and Terrorism, *Terrorism: The Role of Moscow and its Subcontractors*, 97th Cong., 1st sess., June 26, 1982, p. 11.

[113] See Moss's testimony in *Role of Moscow*, pp. 11, 49.

[114] *Ibid.*

I can affirm that...in my experience with Cuban officials during four years of service in the government, the relationship was never one of respect between Cubans and Nicaraguans. The Cubans always spoke as if they were the bosses. They were always very arrogant and demanding. They do not suggest in Nicaragua, they order in Nicaragua.[115]

The Cuban military and security advisers who are reported to be stationed in Nicaragua, numbering between 2,500 and 3,000, are known to operate at all levels of the government and the Sandinista People's Army (EPS).[116] The Cubans in Nicaragua constitute a de facto ruling class, even controlling who enters and leaves the country. According to Farach, Nicaragua's Office of Immigration and Naturalization "is absolutely controlled by Cuban government officials."[117] Sandinista defector Alvaro Baldizón confirmed that Cuban influence in Nicaragua's Interior Ministry (MINT) is extensive and Cuban advice and observations are treated as though they were orders.[118] (The MINT is the regime's law enforcement/internal security arm and is regarded as an EPS component.)

Castro's Nicaraguan "robot" is more than willing to do its fair share of "revolutionary internationalism." Articles 8 and 9 of Nicaragua's Socialist Constitution indicate the regime's expansionist intentions by declaring that the Nicaraguan people are an "integral part of the Central American nation" and that Nicaragua will spare no efforts to achieve "political and economic integration" in the region—i.e., to export the Nicaraguan revolution.[119]

---

[115] From his testimony in U.S. Congress, Senate, Committee on Labor and Human Resources, Subcommittee on Alcoholism and Drug Abuse, *Drugs and Terrorism*, 1984 98th Cong., 2d sess., August 2, 1984, pp. 83-84.

[116] U.S. Departments of State and Defense, *Background Paper: Nicaragua's Military Build-Up and Support For Central American Subversion*, July 18, 1984, p. 11.

[117] *Drugs and Terrorism*, pp. 83-84.

[118] U.S. Department of State, *Inside the Sandinista Regime: A Special Investigator's Perspective* (Washington, D.C.: USGPO, February 1986), p. 16.

[119] As pointed out by Bruce Fein and Albert Blaustein, "Nicaragua's Constitution: Echos of Mein Kampf," *Freedom at Issue*, March/April 1987, p. 38.

The Cubans, by operating within the Nicaraguan military, intelligence, and security services (created as virtual clones of their Cuban counterparts) have expertly concealed the extent of their efforts to support and direct destabilization activities throughout Latin America. By mid-1980, the principal Nicaraguan agencies used by the Cubans to coordinate "national liberation" efforts in the region had been established (see Figure 3).

The FSLN's International Relations Directorate (DRI), which was closely modeled after the DA, represents the FSLN's 12-member ruling National Directorate, particularly in its dealings with other Communist states and

Figure 3: Nicaragua's Security Apparatus

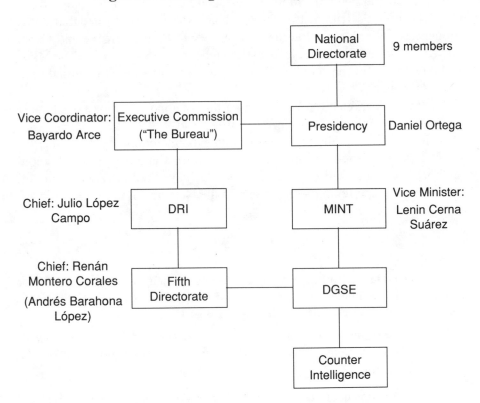

[Sources: Based in part on a more extensive diagram prepared by Jiri and Virginia Valenta, "Sandinistas in Power," *Problems of Communism* (Sep/Oct 1985), p. 28; and on other sources as cited in text.]

revolutionary movements.[120] The DRI is also responsible for establishing and maintaining support networks for the General Directorate of State Security (DGSE), which is the Sandinista secret police, and the Fifth Directorate of Intelligence, which is Nicaragua's "DGI." Cuba's assistance in support of Nicaragua's guerrilla support apparatus included setting up Cuban-style front companies for acquiring arms and munitions.[121] The Fifth Directorate is headed by "Renán Montero Corrales," the DA agent whose real name is reportedly Andrés Barahona López.[122] Also identified by the pseudonym "the old man," Barahona was a colonel in the Cuban intelligence service and alleged comrade-in-arms of Ché Guevara in Bolivia. Castro Hidalgo noted in his book that "Renán," "served as a liaison between the DGI and Guevara in Bolivia."[123] According to Bolaños, Barahona was ordered to work with the FSLN in the late 1960s. Barahona served as an assistant to DA official Julian López Díaz during the FSLN's war against Somoza in the late 1970s. Tomás Borge, who became the Sandinista regime's interior minister, was so pleased with Barahona's work that he asked Fidel Castro to allow him to remain permanently in Nicaragua.[124] After the FSLN takeover, Barahona was redocumented as a Nicaraguan citizen and made de facto head of the DGSE.[125]

DRI chief Julio López Campo reports directly to the National Directorate, just as Piñeiro reports directly to Fidel Castro. According to Bolaños, "Montero" coordinates with López Campo on a daily basis on all important political affairs.[126] The other Cuban advisers to the DRI are all DA personnel.[127]

---

[120] Bolaños interview, *op cit*, p. 317.

[121] Fontaine, "Cuban-backed fronts," *op cit*.

[122] U.S. Department of State, *"Revolution Beyond Our Borders": Sandinista Intervention in Central America*, Special Report No. 132, September 1985, p. 4.

[123] Castro Hidalgo, *Spy for Fidel, op cit*, p. 101.

[124] "Inside Communist Nicaragua: The Miguel Bolaños Transcripts," *Backgrounder* (The Heritage Foundation), no. 294, September 30, 1983, p. 8.

[125] U.S. Department of State, Bureau of Public Affairs, *Strategic Situation in Central America and the Caribbean*, Current Policy no. 352, December 14, 1981, p. 6.

[126] *Hydra of Carnage*, p. 317

[127] *Ibid*.

Aspillaga affirmed that, "All of the key advisers in the Nicaraguan government, including the chief of intelligence, known by the code-name 'the old man' [Barahona] are Cuban intelligence officers."

The 4,000-member DGSE, which Bolaños noted was ten times the size of the late Somoza's secret police, has specific responsibility for all cases involving national security and counter-revolutionary activity. Bolaños described it as modeled after Cuba's State Security Department (DSE) and DGI.[128] He added that the DGSE staff in 1983 included 400 Cubans, seventy Russians, forty to fifty East Germans, and twenty to twenty-five Bulgarians.[129] The Soviets reportedly concentrated on intelligence operations, while the Cubans concerned themselves with counterintelligence.[130] Cuban Brigadier General Rafael del Pino, who defected to the United States in May 1987, confirmed that some 300 to 400 Cuban advisers in Nicaragua actually were intelligence operatives assigned to create "a Nicaraguan robot" that will follow Cuba's lead in spreading revolution.[131] Moscow-trained Lenin Cerna Suárez headed the DGSE's counterintelligence department from its inception until 1988, answering to Vice Interior Minister Luís Carrión Cruz, who was theoretically responsible for the entire Nicaraguan security apparatus.[132] Bolaños affirmed, however, that a Cuban general ("Roberto") exercised "100-percent control" over all the Cuban advisers in Nicaragua, as well as the Nicaraguan security apparatus.[133] In March 1988, Cerna was appointed to Carrión's position as MINT vice minister.[134]

---

[128] "Nicaragua's Secret Police," *Foreign Report*, December 5, 1985, p. 1; and Bolaños interview, *Hydra*, p. 314.

[129] Don Oberdorfer and Joanne Omang, "Nicaragua Bares Plan to Discredit Foes," *Washington Post*, June 19, 1983, p. A1.

[130] Jiri and Virginia Valenta, "Sandinistas in Power," *Problems of Communism*, September/October 1985, p. 12, citing an interview with Bolaños.

[131] *Washington Times*, June 30, 1987, citing the General's Radio Martí interviews.

[132] For an example of Cerna's brutal interrogation techniques, see the testimony of a victim in the U.S. Department of State, *Human Rights in Nicaragua Under the Sandinistas: From Revolution to Repression*, 1986, p. 83.

[133] Bolaños interview, *Hydra*, p. 312.

[134] *FBIS*, vol. 6, March 7, 1988, p. 11, citing Managua Domestic Service.

The Directorate commander who oversees Nicaraguan subversive activities is Bayardo Arce, also vice coordinator of its Executive Commission. Arce's "Bureau" is actually a clandestine government agency through which the Sandinista leaders and their Cuban advisers support guerrilla and terrorist groups throughout the region. Arce maintains close contact with the Soviet bloc. He returned to Managua on March 16, 1988, after visiting Bulgaria, Czechoslovakia, the Soviet Union, Poland, Yugoslavia, and the German Democratic Republic to update unspecified "cooperation and assistance agreements."[135] He also hosts visiting representatives of foreign terrorist organizations. For example, he met in Managua on June 25, 1987, with a delegation of the Palestine Liberation Organization (PLO).[136]

Nicaragua serves as a support center not only for Central American extremists, but also for South American, West European, and Middle Eastern terrorist organizations. About thirty "internationalist" groups reportedly have offices or representatives in Nicaragua and form part of the support system for subversion and terrorism in Latin America.[137] The DRI is responsible for maintaining contact with members of foreign terrorist organizations in Nicaragua, such as the Basque Fatherland and Freedom (ETA) and the Italian Red Brigades.[138]

The DA and DGI undoubtedly use Cuban diplomatic offices in Nicaragua as operational centers for directing Cuba's destabilization programs in Central America. With more than 100 staffers, the Cuban embassy in Managua is said to be larger than any Western embassy in that capital, and the Cubans operate at least three consulates around the country.[139] In fact, those who have held the Cuban ambassadorial post in Nicaragua have been DA agents.[140] DA official

---

[135] *FBIS*, vol. 6, March 18, 1988, p. 23, citing *La Prensa* [Managua], March 15, 1988, p. 1.

[136] *FBIS*, vol. 6, July 16, 1986, p. I5, citing *Radio Sandino*.

[137] *Background Paper*, p. 31; and Juan O. Tamayo, "World's Leftists Find a Haven in Nicaragua," *Miami Herald*, March 3, 1985, p. A1.

[138] Bolaños, *Hydra*, p. 316.

[139] Dennis Volman, "What the Cubans are doing in Nicaragua," *Christian Science Monitor*, November 23, 1984.

[140] Bolaños interview, *Hydra*, p. 315.

Julián López Díaz served as Cuban ambassador to Nicaragua from July 1979 to October 1987, when he was replaced by Norberto Hernández Curbelo, a DA vice chief.[141]

Five days after the presidents of Central America signed the Central America peace plan in August 1987, Daniel Ortega went to Havana to consult with Castro on the agreement and the future of Cuban advisers in Nicaragua.[142] The fact that Ortega was accompanied by DRI chief Julio López and met with both Castro and Piñeiro indicated that the subject of peace was not a priority topic on the agenda.[143] In early November 1987, Daniel Ortega reminded the world where his true sympathies lie by traveling to Moscow to attend the Soviet Union's 70th anniversary celebrations and the Party Congress meeting. During a stopover in Havana enroute to Moscow, Ortega again met with Piñeiro.[144] Cuba's new ambassador to Nicaragua, Norberto Hernández, was also present for what appeared to be a DA strategy session with Cuba's Nicaraguan puppet.

VII. EXPORTING THE NICARAGUAN MODEL

To ascertain how the DA, with the aid of its Nicaraguan surrogate, has fared in its efforts to systemize the political-military model of guerrilla warfare elsewhere in Latin America since 1979, individual country assessments follow.

CENTRAL AMERICA

El Salvador

Soon after Somoza's ouster, the DA support network in Costa Rica shifted its activities toward support of Salvadoran guerrilla groups by establishing training camps and the beginning of arms supply systems in Costa Rica, Honduras, and Nicaragua.[145] The principal DA coordinator for this effort,

---

[141] *Granma*, October 14, 1987, p. 1.

[142] *Washington Post*, August 13, 1987, p. A32.

[143] USIA, Radio Martí Program, *Quarterly Situation Report,* Third Quarter 1987, pp. 17-18.

[144] *Granma*, November 2, 1987, p. 1.

[145] State Dept., *Cuba's Renewed Support*, p. 6.

Fernando Comas Pérez, operated first out of the secret DA operations center in San José, Costa Rica, and later directly from the Cuban consulate, where he held the title of vice consul.

After El Salvador's right-wing military regime was overthrown in a reformist civil-military coup on October 15, 1979, unification of the five Salvadoran guerrilla groups became Cuba's priority. By May 1980, Castro had pressured the Salvadoran Communist Party (PCES) and rebel leaders into forming the Unified Revolutionary Directorate (DRU) to serve as the high command for political-military planning.[146] Advisers from the Cuban MININT's DOE then began helping DRU leaders with initial war plans that summer.[147]

Cuban efforts to force the Salvadoran rebels to take the bigger step of establishing a united guerrilla front faltered because of persistent rivalries and less than unanimous approval of the growing Cuban role. In August 1980, the Armed Forces of National Resistance (FARN), then headed by Ernesto Jovel, withdrew from the DRU over a dispute with Joaquín Villalobos of the People's Revolutionary Army (ERP). The dispute was settled after Jovel's private plane plunged into the Pacific on September 22 while enroute to Panama.[148] The FARN, under Jovel's pro-Cuban successor, José Eduardo Sancho Castañeda ("Fermán Cienfuegos"), rejoined the DRU, thereby enabling the formation that fall of the Farabundo Martí National Liberation Front (FMLN) and a resumption of Cuban arms shipments. According to Arquimedes Canadas, a former FMLN guerrilla field commander ("Alejandro Montenegro") who defected in May 1983, "The Cubans killed him [Jovel] because he was always openly opposed to Cuba's plans."[149] Canadas also explained that it was Cuban policy to sanction the assassination of rebel leaders who resisted Cuban pressure to unify and submit to Cuban direction.[150]

As amply documented by the U.S. State Department, the Cubans directed

---

[146] "Leftist Organizations Send Message to Castro," *FBIS*, vol. 6, May 30, 1980, pp. P7-P9.

[147] State Dept., *Cuba's Renewed Support*, p. 6.

[148] "Organization and Evolution of the Salvadoran Insurgent Movement," *Bulletin of the U.S. Department of State* (May 1982), p. 75.

[149] *Ibid.*

[150] State and Defense Depts., *Background Paper*, p. 17, citing Canadas's interview with State Department officials on March 12, 1984.

the major flow of U.S.-made arms from Vietnam to the FMLN between October 1980 and February 1981.[151] DA official Fernando Comas coordinated the FMLN arms supply operation from the Cuban consulate in San José, using a Costa Rican-based air express company operated by Fernando Carrasco, a member of the Chilean MIR.[152]

Since 1981, Cuba is known to have supported—with training, arms, and munitions—several major operations carried out by the FMLN. These have included the bombing of the Golden Bridge in October 1981, the sabotage of seventy-five percent of the Salvadoran Air Force at the Ilopango Air Base in January 1982, and the bloody assault on the 4th Brigade Headquarters in El Paraiso in December 1983. Adin Inglés Alvarado, a guerrilla captain until his defection in early 1985, stated that he and twenty-seven other rebels went to Cuba to plan and train for that attack.[153] He added that Cuba supplied the weapons and ammunition used in the raid (in which 100 soldiers were killed). "Besides the training," he said, "they gave us all the material to use. The explosives, machine-guns, and ammunition were totally sent from Cuba. Nicaragua was only the conduit, or staging point."

Another senior rebel defector, Napoleón Romero, affirmed in a press interview in April 1985 that, "Nicaragua is a directional center of the FMLN...there they give us advice, the Sandinistas as well as the Cubans."[154] Salvadoran guerrilla documents, captured in 1985, provided evidence of assistance given the FMLN by Cuba, Nicaragua, the Soviet Union, Bulgaria, and Vietnam.[155] Manuel Piñeiro, apparently alluding to reports that Cuba had reduced its arms support of the FMLN, told a visiting U.S. official in early 1985 that Cuba would continue its aid to the FMLN and other guerrilla forces in

---

[151] See U.S. Department of State, Bureau of Public Affairs, *Communist Interference in El Salvador*, Special Report No. 80, February 23, 1981.

[152] State Dept., *Revolution Beyond*, p. 17.

[153] Tom Díaz, "Salvadoran Rebel Defectors Reveal Cuba, Managua Roles," *Washington Times,* May 21, 1985.

[154] "Salvadoran Rebel Leader Cites Cuban, Managua Aid," *Washington Times*, April 30, 1985, p. 5.

[155] James LeMoyne, "Captured Salvadoran Rebel Papers List Training Classes Overseas," *New York Times*, May 21, 1985, p. 11.

Latin America and will do nothing to undercut the FMLN or the Sandinista regime.[156]

On June 19, 1985, the Cuban-advised FMLN launched a new terrorist campaign against the U.S. presence in El Salvador when urban commandos of the Revolutionary Party of Central American Workers (PRTC) machine-gunned to death four U.S. Marine embassy guards and nine civilians—including two U.S. businessmen, a Chilean, two Guatemalans, and four Salvadoreans—and wounded 15 others at a sidewalk café in San Salvador. In October 1985, the FMLN staged two other major operations that must have required Cuban approval: a raid on a Salvadoran army garrison housing U.S. trainers and the kidnapping of President José Napoleón Duarte's daughter. Negotiations for her release were channeled through Managua. In order to win her freedom, President Duarte capitulated and provided safe conduct out of the country to 104 wounded guerrillas and twenty-two others. Piñeiro received the rebels on their arrival at the Havana airport.[157]

Piñeiro initiated Cuba's 1987 campaign of support for the FMLN by attending an FMLN/PCES "solidarity meeting" in Havana in January.[158] On March 31, FMLN guerrillas again overran the 4th Brigade Headquarters, killing at least sixty-four soldiers and a U.S. military trainer. President Duarte stated in a television interview that this attack may also have been planned with Cuban technical assistance and training because of the greatly increased accuracy of the guerrilla mortar barrage on the garrison.[159] Duarte told a U.S. congressional delegation in September that the Sandinista regime had "dramatically increased" shipments of military hardware to the FMLN since the Central American peace proposal was initiated.[160] The FMLN country-wide offensive in the fall of 1988 featured another bloody attack on the El Paraiso garrison, as well as car bombings and a mortar attack in San Salvador.

---

[156] Roger Fontaine, "Castro Says Military Aid to Rebels in Salvador Will Go On," *Washington Times*, April 18, 1985.

[157] "Manuel Piñeiro Receives Group," *FBIS*, vol. 6, October 28, 1985, p. Q2, citing Havana Television Service.

[158] *Granma*, January 24, 1987, p. 1.

[159] "President Duarte on Cuban Involvement in Attack," *FBIS*, vol. 6, April 13, 1987, p. P4, citing a San Salvador television report.

[160] *Washington Times*, September 10, 1987.

Guatemala

In the spring of 1980, DA agents began to actively press the four main Guatemalan guerrilla factions to unify to qualify for increased Cuban aid. That June, the rebel leaders sent a letter to Fidel Castro reporting that, as a result of their first meeting in Managua, they agreed "to do everything necessary" to achieve unity and to coordinate their military activities.[161] By signing an agreement in Managua on November 2, the guerrilla leaders initiated the process to establish the Guatemalan National Revolutionary Union (URNG), under an executive directorate called the General Revolutionary Command. Piñeiro, together with Ramiro Abreu Quintana, an official of the DA's Central America Section, represented Castro at the signing ceremony.[162] The guerrilla leaders then traveled to Havana to present the accord to Castro.

The URNG itself was not formally established until February 1982.[163] By 1985, operational cooperation among URNG forces appeared to have increased as they inflicted growing numbers of casualties on the Guatemalan Army in isolated rural areas. In 1988, URNG forces continued to wage Central America's second most active Castroite insurgency.

Honduras

In 1980, the Sandinista regime began to provide logistical support, training, and advice for the Castroite Honduran extremist groups, primarily in order to incorporate them into the logistics network for the transfer of arms to the FMLN in El Salvador.[164] One pro-Cuban group, the Lorenzo Zelaya Popular Revolutionary Front (FPR-LZ), ambushed a vehicle in which five U.S. military advisers were riding in Tegucigalpa on September 23, 1981, wounding two of them. Documents captured in a police raid on a safe-house of the Honduran Front for Popular Liberation (FHLP) in Tegucigalpa on November 17, 1981, indicated that the FHLP was created in Nicaragua by high-level Sandinista leaders, was headquartered in Managua, and its members received

---

[161] *Granma Weekly Review*, June 8, 1980, p. 1.

[162] State Dept., *Cuba's Renewed Support*, p. 7.

[163] "Guatemala's Four Main Rebel Groups Join Forces," *New York Times*, March 3, 1982.

[164] "State Dept., *Revolution Beyond*, p. 13.

military training in Nicaragua and Cuba.[165] Members of other Honduran terrorist groups who perpetrated aircraft hijacking and hostage-taking operations in the 1981-82 period were given sanctuary in Cuba. The promise of more significant Cuban support inspired the three main Honduran terrorist groups to coordinate under the National Unity Directorate of the Revolutionary Movement of Honduras (DNU-MRH) in March 1983. The Honduran Army defeated two attempts by rebels—trained and supported by Cuba and Nicaragua—to establish a base for rural insurgency in the country in 1983-84. Since then, occasional raids by security forces against terrorist safe-houses in Honduran cities have indicated continued organizational activity.[166] In April 1985, seven agents of the Nicaraguan DGSE were captured inside Honduras and confessed to their role in supplying arms to subversive groups in Honduras.[167] In July 1988, the Cinchonero Popular Liberation Movement (MPL), citing "the heroic people of Vietnam, Cuba, and Nicaragua," claimed responsibility for an attack on a group of off-duty U.S. soldiers. [168]

Costa Rica

In early May 1981, Costa Rica suspended consular relations with Cuba over charges of arms smuggling, and expelled the Cubans assigned to the Cuban consulate in San José, including DA regional coordinator Fernando Comas.[169] The action followed an unprecedented outbreak of terrorism in Costa Rica by an international Marxist-Leninist group now known as the New Republic Movement (MRN), whose leader has close ties to Cuba and Nicaragua.[170] The Cubans then unleashed their Sandinista surrogates. Sandinista agents staged

---

[165] *Ibid.*

[166] See Guy Gugliotta, "Cuba Trains Guerrillas at Secret Military Base," *Miami Herald*, September 11, 1983, p. A1; "Sandinistas, Cuba Training Guerrillas, Honduran Says," *Miami Herald*, January 24, 1984; and Loren Jenkins, "Honduran Army Defeats Cuban-Trained Rebel Unit," *Washington Post*, November 22, 1983, p. A1.

[167] State Dept., *Revolution Beyond*, p. 15.

[168] *FBIS*, vol. 6, July 22, 1988, p. 22. Citing *ACAN*.

[169] *FBIS*, vol. 6, May 15, 1981, p. P1; May 28, 1981, pp. P9-P10; and September 14, 1983, p. P3.

[170] State Dept., *Revolution Beyond*, p. 17.

or attempted to carry out several terrorist actions in Costa Rica in the 1981-82 period.[171] Sandinista-supported groups also conducted a series of attacks in Costa Rica between 1981 and 1985. On March 17, 1981, one of these terrorist commandos, "The Family," blew up a van in which three U.S. Marine embassy guards were riding in San José, seriously wounding one of them.

Cuba and Nicaragua have continued to prepare the groundwork for future "armed struggle" in Costa Rica. According to the Costa Rican Ministry of Public Security, by July 1985 at least 700 Costa Rican leftists had received military training in Cuba over the previous four years, and most already had returned to their country through Nicaragua.[172] Major elements of the orthodox Costa Rican CP, the Popular Vanguard Party (PVP), have gained military experience fighting anti-Sandinista rebels in Nicaragua since the early 1980s and have continued to provide permanent training services for paramilitary cadres who return to Costa Rica.[173] Former Sandinista security official Baldizón confirmed the training of PVP members in southern Nicaragua for six-month periods.[174] After a five-year lull, anti-U.S. terrorism reappeared in San José in April 1988 when a terrorist tossed a powerful fragmentation grenade at several persons in front of the American-Costa Rican Cultural Center, wounding two U.S. women—one seriously—and four other persons.

Panama

The DA has used Panama to facilitate Cuban support for guerrilla groups in Central America. Piñeiro apparently has longstanding ties to Panama Defense Forces (PDF) Commander Manuel Antonio Noriega. In November 1975, Piñeiro headed a high-level Cuban mission to Panama and met with top Panamanian government officials, including Noriega, then the G-2 (intelligence) chief.[175] That year, Piñeiro was advising the late Panamanian dictator General

---

[171] *Ibid*, pp. 17-18.

[172] "Deputy Minister on Leftists Training in Cuba," *FBIS*, vol. 6, July 30, 1985, citing *La Nación* [San José], July 21, 1985.

[173] State Dept., *Revolution Beyond*, p. 16.

[174] U.S. Department of State, *Inside the Sandinista Regime: A Special Investigator's Perspective*, February 1986, p. 17.

[175] *FBIS*, vol. 6, November 28, 1975, citing Panama City Television.

Omar Torrijos in negotiating the Panama Canal Treaties.[176] During 1978-79, the DA made extensive use of Panama to ferry arms to the FSLN guerrilla forces in Costa Rica and Nicaragua. As DA operations chief, Luís Hernández Ojeda coordinated FSLN operations from Panama and maintained direct contact with Piñeiro in Havana.[177] Piñeiro attended Torrijos' funeral in Panama in August 1981.[178] By that time, Cuba maintained its second largest embassy in Panama City and it reportedly has served as a focal point for Soviet-Cuban coordination of revolutionary activities in the region.[179] Aspillaga charged that Cuba's MININT Minister José Abrantes Fernández has had a close association with Noriega, through whom Cuba has supplied arms to Nicaragua and guerrillas in El Salvador and Honduras, as well as in Colombia.[180] In September 1982, Piñeiro accompanied Cuban Politburo member Osmany Cienfuegos on another official visit to Panama.[181] In 1983, according to Jay Mallin, the DA post in Panama was staffed by about a half dozen DA officials and was responsible for Colombia and for serving as a link to Central American operations.[182]

According to the U.S. Department of Commerce, about twenty of the sixty Cuban front companies operating in Panama in 1986 had been involved with providing weapons to Latin American guerrilla groups.[183] Aspillaga affirmed

---

[176] See, for example, *FBIS*, vol. 6, June 12, 1975, p. N1.

[177] Jay Mallin, "Cuba Unit Fans Flames in Latin America," *Washington Times*, August 26, 1983, p. 5A.

[178] FBIS, vol. 6, August 4, 1981, p. N7, citing the French Press Agency.

[179] Valentas, "Soviet Strategies in the Region," p. 112, citing *La República* [Panama City], October 16, 1981.

[180] Lewis H. Diuguid, "Chilean Officials Waste Funds, Defector Says," *Washington Post*, August 11, 1987; and John McCaslin, "Intelligence Officer Who Defected Says Castro Lives in Lap of Luxury," *Washington Times*, August 11, 1987.

[181] *Latin America Weekly Report*, October 1, 1982, p. 4.

[182] Jay Mallin, "Cuban Intelligence Elite Pushes Subversion in Americas," *Washington Times*, August 25, 1983, p. 7A.

[183] Roger Fontaine, "Cuba-backed Fronts Evade U.S. Embargo," *Washington Times*, May 23, 1986, p. 1A.

that Noriega helped Havana to purchase and send weapons to guerrilla groups in El Salvador, Honduras, and Colombia, as well as to Nicaragua.[184] CIMEX, one of the Panamanian trading companies set up by Cuban agents, played a central role in arranging some of the arms purchases.

In February 1988, a federal grand jury in Miami indicted Noriega for drug trafficking and racketeering. As a result, the United States finally began pressuring the corrupt dictator to leave Panama, emboldening the political opposition in Panama to also clamor for his departure, at least until the regime cracked down on it. Finding himself increasingly isolated, Noriega turned to the Cubans for help. High-level Cuban intelligence officers reportedly began visiting Noriega to advise him on how to deal with the situation and calm tensions within the PDF.[185]

By mid-March 1988, Noriega and the Cubans reportedly were operating a secret arms airlift from Havana to three locations in Panama and outside the control of the PDF, with the intent of building an infrastructure for waging guerrilla war, according to Major Augusto Villalaz, a Panamanian Air Force officer who was granted political asylum in the United States that month.[186] Villalaz revealed that he personally made three flights from Cuba into Panama to deliver weapons requested by Noriega; each flight carried sixteen tons of military equipment, including 100,000 AK-47 assault rifles, rocket-propelled grenades, hand-grenades, and ammunition. Villalaz added that a total of sixteen flights carrying about 500,000 pounds of weapons were planned.[187] Eduardo Arango, ousted President Eric Delvalle's consul general in London, charged that the weapons shipments were being unloaded by Panamanian political cadres and technicians who had been trained "by the hundreds" in Cuba and the Soviet Union over the years.[188] Cubans and allied guerrilla forces

---

[184] Joe Pichirallo, "Cuba Used Noriega to Obtain High-Tech U.S. Goods, Defector Says," *Washington Post,* August 12, 1987, p. A7.

[185] *Washington Times*, February 8, 1988, p. A10.

[186] Lena Williams, "Defecting Panamanian Pilot Says Noriega Is Storing Cuban Arms," *Washington Post*, March 21, 1988.

[187] James M. Dorsey, "Cuba Helps Plant Seeds of War," *Washington Times*, March 21, 1988.

[188] Lou Marano, "Panamanian Envoys Ask U.S. to Send Troops," *Washington Times,* March 23, 1988, p. A11.

also reportedly began arriving in Panama.[189] By mid-April, the infiltrators had increased to 1,800 Cubans and Nicaraguans, although confirmation was lacking.[190]

Also by that month, Noriega reportedly was becoming increasingly reliant on Cuban military advisers.[191] The DA had reportedly established a political unit in Panama to advise Noriega.[192] Among its members were "Luís Arbezu" (sic) (probably DA vice chief José Antonio Arbesú Fraga); DA vice chief Fernando Ravelo, who coordinated Colombian M-19 support for Noriega; Ramiro Abreu Quintana, the DA's Central American Section chief; José Luís Ojalvo; and CEAL official Luís Hernández Ojeda.[193] Arbesu, reputed to be an expert in manipulating the U.S. political system and media, presumably was advising the less astute Panamanian dictator on ways of countering the U.S. pressure campaign against him.

Nicaraguan security officials were reported to be serving a role in Panama similar to that of Cuba. Bayardo Arce reportedly was directing the Nicaraguan operation from Managua, while Ricardo Wheelock, an intelligence chief, was directing Nicaraguan "military" efforts in Panama and serving as a liaison between Noriega and Nicaraguan Defense Minister Humberto Ortega. DRI chief Julio López and Vice Interior Minister Lenin Cerna also reportedly were operating in Panama under the direction of Arce and Wheelock, respectively.[194]

[189] Lou Marano, "Marxist Brigade Infiltrates Panama to Defend Noriega," *Washington Times*, April 5, 1988, p. A1.

[190] James M. Dorsey and Lou Marano, "Cuban Presence Grows in Panama," *Washington Times*, April 14, 1988, p. A1.

[191] David E. Pitt, "Noriega Reported to Be 'Leaning Heavily' on Cuban Advisers," *New York Times*, April 1988.

[192] "Cuban Presence Grows," *op cit*.

[193] "Cuban Presence Grows," *op cit*; DA positions added from CIA Directory, June 1987, pp. 7-8.

[194] "Cuban Presence Grows," *op cit*.

THE CARIBBEAN

Jamaica

Having made former Prime Minister Michael Manley's close relations with Cuba a major issue during the 1980 election campaign, Edward Seaga—in his first official act as prime minister in January 1981—terminated Cuba's programs in Jamaica. Seaga also expelled the 500 or so Cubans working on the island, including Cuban Ambassador Armando Ulises Estrada, a DA vice chief, for his involvement in an arms smuggling operation.[195] Although the Seaga government stopped short of severing diplomatic ties with Cuba at that time and allowed a few Cuban embassy officials to remain, it broke relations on October 29, 1981. In a further action in November 1983, Seaga expelled a Cuban journalist and four Soviet diplomats, whom he identified as KGB agents, for espionage and conspiracy to murder a protocol officer at the Jamaican Ministry of Foreign Affairs.[196]

Cuba's Grenada setback of October 1983 strained relations with the local Moscow-line, violence-oriented CP, the Workers Party of Jamaica (WPJ), which was critical of Castro's unsupportive attitude toward the Marxist-Leninist hard-liners who ousted and assassinated Prime Minister Maurice Bishop, a friend of Castro's.[197] Cuban-WPJ relations began to improve, however, by November 1984, when Cuban representatives attended the WPJ's fifth-anniversary ceremony in Kingston.[198] In recent years, the WPJ has been implicated in several major bank robberies. Other subversive acts perpetrated by unidentified groups have included raids on police stations.

Grenada

Reports of Cuban participation in the expertly planned and executed overthrow of Eric Gairy's unpopular regime by a few dozen members of Maurice Bishop's New Jewel Movement (NJM) in March 1979 were never

---

[195] State Dept. *Cuba's Renewed Support*, p. 9.

[196] *Congressional Record*, June 18, 1987, p. H5245.

[197] Carl Stone, "The WPJ and the PNP," *Daily Gleaner* [Kingston], December 24, 1984.

[198] "Cuba Accepts Invitation to Attend WPJ Congress," *FBIS*, vol. 6, November 29, 1984, pp. S4-S5, citing *CANA*.

substantiated. Nevertheless, one early Cuban connection was Oscar Cárdenas Junquera, a DA official who worked with the NJM in Grenada before the coup.[199] After Grenada's opening of diplomatic relations with Cuba on April 14, 1979, another senior DA official, Julián Torres Rizo, was sent to Grenada as the Cuban ambassador in order to supervise Cuba's programs in Grenada.[200] According to DGI defector Gerardo Peraza, Torres Rizo had served as one of the most active DGI officers in both Cuba and the United States.[201] Torres Rizo also had served as Cuba's ambassador to Dominica and St. Lucia.[202]

With their virtual carte blanche in Grenada, the Cubans and Soviets made the island the focal point of anti-democratic activities in the Eastern Caribbean. The 35,000 pounds of secret NJM and Cuban documents captured in the occupation of Grenada in late October 1983 yielded some documentary evidence of the close subversive collaboration among the DA, NJM, and FSLN. For example, one report in Spanish on Nicaragua and the Socialist International (SI), signed by Piñeiro, shows how the NJM and Sandinista activists, acting under DA direction, sought to undermine the regional SI meeting held in Managua on January 6-7, 1983.[203] Another document, also signed by Piñeiro, is a secret NJM-PCC agreement providing for the training of Grenadians in Cuba.[204]

In addition to Torres Rizo, two other DA officials were reported to be in Grenada at the time of the military action. Carlos Díaz Larrañaga, who had arrived on the island only a day earlier, was one of the twenty-four Cubans killed in the fighting.[205] The other DA agent, Gastón Díaz Evarista, previously

[199] U.S. Department of State, *Grenada: A Preliminary Report*, December 16, 1983, p. 7.

[200] State Dept., *Cuba's Renewed Support*, p. 10.

[201] Congress, *The Role of Cuba*, pp. 14-15; and Robert Moss, "Capitol Hill Visitor Is a Spy for Castro," *The London Daily Telegraph*, September 3, 1979.

[202] CIA, *Directory*, p. 226.

[203] U.S. Departments of State and Defense, *Grenada Documents: An Overview and Selections*, September 1984, Documents #33, 39.

[204] *Ibid.*, Doc. #17.

[205] *Granma*, November 14, 1983, p. 8.

had served in Barbados and on the DA's Jamaica desk.[206] Since the U.S. intervention in Grenada in 1983, however, Cuba has maintained a low profile in its subversive efforts in the Eastern Caribbean.

SOUTH AMERICA

Suriname

Suriname was an economically prosperous, five-year old democracy when Sergeant Desire "Desi" Bouterse seized power in a February 25, 1980, coup. Under Bouterse's repressive and incompetent rule, the former Dutch colony became South America's "Angola." Cuban activities in support of Bouterse's security and military forces began growing after the arrival in September 1982 of the new Cuban ambassador, Oscar Cárdenas.[207] A PCC member and former head of the DA's Central American Section, Cárdenas was an unusually high-ranking ambassador for a country as small as Suriname. He was also described as a highly successful DGI operator.[208] Only three months after his arrival, Bouterse's Cuban-trained and -advised security forces rounded up and massacred fifteen prominent political opponents under the pretext of a coup attempt. With the subsequent cut-off of Dutch assistance to Suriname, Cuban influence increased. During the year that he spent in Paramaribo, Cárdenas reportedly became involved in almost every aspect of government business.[209] He also maintained close ties to the Marxist-oriented People's Revolutionary Party (RVP).[210] Cuban advisers—allowed to come and go freely—trained Bouterse's personal bodyguard and advised the Suri-

---

[206] CIA, *Directory*, pp. 8, 223, 229.

[207] Don Bonning, "Suriname Denies It's Edging Into Havana's Caribbean Orbit," *Miami Herald*, January 19, 1983.

[208] David S. Harvey, "Suriname: Cuba's New Conquest," *Defense & Foreign Affairs*, November 1983, p. 40.

[209] James LeMoyne, "Strongman Finds Suriname Isn't Easily Subdued," *New York Times*, January 19, 1984.

[210] Edward Dew, "Did Suriname Switch?" *Caribbean Review*, vol.12, no. 2 (Fall 1983), p. 29.

name Ministries of Information and People's Mobilization.[211]

Coincidentally, on the same day as the joint Caribbean/U.S. intervention in Grenada on October 25, 1983, Bouterse, fearful that he could suffer the same fate that befell his friend Maurice Bishop, expelled the Cubans from Suriname. Although the Bouterse regime announced a few weeks later that it placed a high priority on improving relations with Havana, the Cubans apparently turned their subversive attentions elsewhere.

Colombia

According to the State Department, Fidel Castro decided in early 1979 to allow Cuba to be used as "a bridge and support base" for narcotics traffickers as a means to aid Cuba economically and contribute to the "deterioration of American society."[212] That August, Cuban Ambassador to Colombia and DA Vice Chief Fernando Ravelo Renedo and First Secretary Gonzalo Bassols Suárez, also a DA operative, began developing a relationship with Colombian narcotics trafficker Jaime Guillot Lara.[213] The development of Cuba's Colombian narco-connection coincided with the M-19's takeover of the Dominican Republic embassy in Bogotá in early 1980. The U.S. ambassador to Colombia, Diego Asencio, was among the thirty diplomats taken hostage by the M-19. Asencio notes in his account of the ordeal that almost as soon as he arrived at the embassy, the Soviet bloc envoys started to leave en masse, moments before the terrorist attack.[214] After sixty-one days, the crisis was resolved peacefully with the aid of Ravelo, who arranged for the terrorists,

---

[211] Jackson Diehl, "Suriname Keeps Foreign Policy In Balance," *Washington Post,* October 13, 1983, p. A28.

[212] Edward Cody, "Castro Ties to Drugs Suggested," *Washington Post*, May 1, 1983.

[213] James Michel, Deputy Assistant Secretary of State for Inter-American Affairs, "Additional Submission on Colombian Drug Traffickers and the Cuban Connection," in U.S. Congress, Senate, Judiciary and Foreign Relations Committees, Subcommittees on Security and Terrorism and Western Hemisphere Affairs, *The Cuban Government's Involvement in Facilitating International Drug Traffic*, 98th Cong., 1st sess., April 30, 1983, p. 684.

[214] Diego and Nancy Asencio, *Our Man Is Inside: Outmaneuvering the Terrorists* (Boston: Little, Brown, 1982), p. 7.

their $2.5-million ransom booty, and a dozen diplomatic hostages to be flown by Cubana Airlines directly to Havana. Asencio noted that Manuel Piñeiro was on hand at the Havana airport to officially welcome the terrorists as heroes.[215]

According to the State Department, official Cuban protection of Guillot's drug trafficking network began in the summer of 1980.[216] The additional purpose of the arrangement was to help finance Latin American guerrilla activities, as well as to utilize the capabilities and expertise of the narcotics traffickers to smuggle weapons to the M-19.[217] The DA thereby created a marriage of convenience—albeit a tenuous one—between two unlikely partners in crime, who until then had been deadly enemies.

Ravelo and Bassols were among the four Cuban officials indicted by a federal grand jury in Miami on November 15, 1982, for conspiring to smuggle narcotics into the United States from 1978 to April 1982, using Guillot's trafficking infrastructure. The other two were identified as René Rodríguez Cruz, the ICAP president and a PCC/CC member; and Vice Admiral of the Cuban Navy Aldo Santamaría Cuadrado (a.k.a. "René Baeza Rodríguez"), also a PCC/CC member.[218]

The perilous threat posed to Colombia's democratic system by the narco-guerrilla alliance was demonstrated dramatically on November 6, 1985, when the M-19, desperate for publicity to reaffirm its "vanguard" status and protest the government's peace process, seized Bogotá's Palace of Justice. The M-19 also wanted to destroy extradition records of narcotics traffickers and terrorize the judiciary. It accomplished the latter two objectives, although the Betancur government's unexpected military counterattack resulted in one of the most violent denouements in the annals of terrorist hostage incidents. About fifty hostages, seventeen soldiers and security personnel, and the thirty-five terrorists were killed in the twenty-eight hours of fierce fighting. According

---

[215] Asencio, *Our Man Is Inside*, p. 231.

[216] Michel, *Cuban Government's Involvement*, p. 684.

[217] *Ibid.*, p. 687.

[218] Mary Thorton, "Four Cuban Officials Indicted in Drug Smuggling," *Washington Post*, November 6, 1982, p. A1; and Jim McGee, "U.S. Indicts Four Castro Officials on Drug-Trafficking Conspiracy," *Miami Herald*, November 6, 1982, p. 1.

to hostage witnesses, one of the Cuban-trained leaders of the operation, Andrés Almarales, personally "executed" most of the eleven judges who died in the incident, although confirmation was lacking.

As elsewhere, one of the DA's objectives in Colombia has been to unify the half-dozen or so rebel groups. To this end, DA agents arranged a mid-1980 meeting of representatives of Colombia's various subversive groups in order to discuss a common strategy and tactics. The meeting resulted in increased practical cooperation, if not agreement, on a unified strategy.[219]

The Cubans also began training M-19 members in rural guerrilla warfare tactics in Cuba. In early 1981, some 150 of these Cuban-trained M-19 members were flown to Panama, were armed by the G-2 chief, General Manuel Noriega, and PDF members, and then were shipped by boat through the Panama Canal to two locations on Colombia's Pacific coast.[220] The poorly organized operation failed, however, and most of the rebels were captured and confessed their Cuban sponsorship. After Cuba admitted as much, Colombia suspended diplomatic relations.[221] In September 1984, the DA reportedly informed the M-19 that if it did not merge with the Colombian CP, at least strategically, the M-19 would no longer receive Cuban-Soviet support.[222] Disagreement over acceptance of President Belisario Betancur's peace offer resulted, however, in internecine warfare between groups advocating continued "armed struggle" and the CP-affiliated Revolutionary Armed Forces of Colombia (FARC), the country's largest guerrilla organization. The FARC used the truce to launch a political party and reorganize its guerrilla fronts.

In June 1985, six of the Colombian guerrilla organizations—the M-19, National Liberation Army (ELN), the Maoist Popular Liberation Army (EPL), and three smaller groups—signed a unity of action accord, setting the

---

[219] State Dept., *Cuba's Renewed Support*, p. 10.

[220] Seymour Hersh, "Panama Strongman Said to Trade in Drugs, Arms and Illicit Money—U.S. Aides Also Assert Noriega Helps Leftist Rebels in Colombia," *New York Times*, June 12, 1986.

[221] *Granma Weekly Review*, March 22, 1981, p. 6.

[222] "Cuba Seeks Communist Party, FARC, M-19 Alliance," *FBIS*, vol. 6, October 1984, p. F1, citing *El Tiempo* [Bogotá], October 1, 1984, p. 2A.

stage for a renewed terrorist campaign.[223] The M-19 also led efforts to form the transnational America Battalion with Ecuador's Alfaro Lives (AVC) group; Peru's SL and Tupac Amaru Revolutionary Movement (MRTA); and other groups in Nicaragua, El Salvador, Costa Rica, Panama, Venezuela, and Uruguay.[224]

The entire Colombian guerrilla movement, including the FARC, M-19, ELN, EPL (Camilist Union), the Quintin Lame Command, and the Workers Revolutionary Party (PRT), established the Simón Bolívar Guerrilla Coordinating Board in October 1987.[225] Although unity has continued to elude the Colombian groups, the FARC's thirty guerrilla fronts and those of the other organizations have become a major insurgency threat to the government of democratically elected President Virgilio Barco Vargas.

Six FARC deserters revealed in August 1987 that various FARC fronts have Cuban advisers attached to them.[226] Other deserters reported that Cubans also are working as advisers and instructors for the ELN and are directing its ecologically and economically disastrous sabotage of oil installations.[227] Numerous ELN kidnappings of oil company officials and a powerful ELN car-bomb that blew up in front of the U.S. Occidental Petroleum Company in Bogotá in February 1988 demonstrated the terrorist trend of the ELN campaign.

The kidnapping of President Belasario Betancur's brother, a magistrate, by the ELN in November 1983 provided the first opportunity for Fidel Castro to reveal himself as the godfather of Colombia's terrorist groups. After the kidnapping provoked a storm of national indignation, Castro, at the urging of President Betancur, publically called on the ELN to release its hostage. The

---

[223] "Seven Rebel Groups Sign Unity of Action Accord," *FBIS*, vol. 6, June 27, 1985, p. F1, citing *El Siglo* [Bogotá], June 20, 1985, p. 1.

[224] See, for example, "Three-Nation Rebel Military Front Uncovered," *FBIS*, vol. 6, August 30, 1985, p. F1, citing *AFP*; and "MRTA Confirms Links to Colombians, Ecuadoreans," *FBIS*, vol. 6, March 4, 1986, p. J2, citing *EFE*.

[225] "Guerrilla Groups Unite, Issue Statement," *FBIS*, vol. 6, October 23, 1987, p. 27, citing *La Hora* [Montevideo], October 11, 1987, p. 5.

[226] *El Tiempo*, August 3, 1987, pp. 1A, 9A.

[227] *El Siglo* [Colombia], January 30, 1988, p. 5.

ELN complied almost immediately, dropping all of its ransom demands.

After the M-19 kidnapped presidential candidate and former ambassador to Washington, Alvaro Gómez Hurtado, in May 1988, Colombian officials again had to appeal to Castro. The Colombian press reported that Minister César Gaviria Trujillo travelled to Havana secretly in early July and arranged direct negotiations between the Colombian government and the M-19.[228] The M-19 released Gómez fifteen days later, after further negotiations conducted in Panama.

Ecuador

The AVC, a pro-Cuban Marxist-Leninist organization, carried out kidnappings, assassinations, bombings, and various other terrorist actions following its emergence in August 1983. [229] Although Cuban involvement, if any, was not reported, the Cuban chargé d'affaires in Quito at that time was José Francisco Ross Paz, a DA agent. The AVC targets included the U.S. presence in Ecuador. In May 1984, the AVC threw a small bomb over the U.S. embassy wall in Quito, and another at a U.S. binational center in Guayaquil in June 1985.[230] A clone of the Colombian M-19, the AVC has ties to Nicaragua, Cuba, and Libya. When Ecuadorean police captured AVC leader Rosa Cárdenas in September 1984, she was carrying documents indicating that she had been soliciting $3 million (U.S.) in funds and training support from Nicaragua and Libya.[231] The AVC's links to Nicaragua prompted Ecuador to break diplomatic relations with the Sandinista regime on October 11, 1985. The government also had established that from thirty to forty AVC rebels were trained in Nicaragua between 1979 and 1983. A few other AVC members were trained by the FMLN in El Salvador.[232] By mid-1986, Ecuadorean security

---

[228] See *El Tiempo* and *El Espectador*, July 5, 1988.

[229] For details, see Robert Thomas Baratta, "Political Violence in Ecuador and the AVC," *Terrorism*, vol. 10, no. 3 (1987), pp. 165-174.

[230] Mallin, "Cuban Intelligence Elite," *op cit.*

[231] "Arrested Guerrilla Reveals Vast Subversive Plan," *FBIS*, vol. 6, September 6, 1984, p. G2, citing the German Press Agency.

[232] Roger Fontaine, "Ecuador Ahead in its Battle With Terrorists," *Washington Times*, January 14, 1986; and "Police Say AVC Members Trained in Libya," *FBIS*, vol. 6, December 22, 1986, pp. G1-2.

forces had rendered the AVC ineffective. AVC leaders reportedly held a "summit" in Nicaragua in mid-1987 in an attempt to regroup and reorganize, but in late 1988, the AVC was demanding an amnesty. [233]

Peru

The Cubans and the Sandinistas have been linked to the MRTA, a rapidly expanding Castroite urban terrorist organization that specializes in anti-U.S. actions. The MRTA's suspected Cuban-Nicaraguan connection emerged soon after the group began operating in late 1984. Peruvian security forces raided an MRTA training camp near Cuzco on November 27 and claimed to have seized weapons, olive-drab military uniforms, and medicines identified as having originated in Cuba and Nicaragua.[234] Former MRTA leader Luís Varese Scotto is reported to have fought with the FSLN against the Somoza regime and to have undergone guerrilla training in Cuba in 1981.[235] Furthermore, a Cuban agent, "Erasmo Dupierre," is reported to have arrived in Lima on December 1, 1984, and to have spent a week holding secret meetings with MRTA leaders, particularly Varese, to plan pre-election political-military strategy.[236]

Unlike the SL's often indiscriminate terrorism, MRTA terrorism has been selective. In July 1985, the MRTA announced that it would focus its actions on "imperialist" (i.e., U.S.) targets. For example, in April 1986, the MRTA detonated a car-bomb outside the U.S. ambassador's residence in Lima to protest the U.S. air raid on Libya.[237] MRTA terrorists attacked the U.S. embassy in Lima in early November 1986, bombed the Eastern Airlines office in January 1987, and fired two 60-mm rockets at the residence of the U.S. ambassador in June 1988.

---

[233] "Police Report on Guerrilla 'Summit,'" *FBIS*, vol. 6, June 26, 1987, p. P1, citing the Spanish Press Agency.

[234] *Oiga* [Lima], December 17, 1984, pp. 13-18.

[235] *Ibid.*

[236] *Oiga*, February 4, 1985, pp. 25-27.

[237] *FBIS*, vol. 6, April 22, 1986, p. J1.

Chile

The DA began to reactivate the MIR in the second half of 1979 by stepping up urban guerrilla warfare training of MIR*istas* in Cuba and assisting the highly trained members to reinfiltrate Chile.[238] By late 1980, at least 100 Cuban-trained MIR terrorists had re-entered Chile and resumed "armed propaganda" (terrorism). The Chilean CP (PCCh), for its part, began re-evaluating its traditionally non-violent line after the FSLN's seizure of power in Nicaragua.

During talks in Havana in December 1980, Fidel Castro and Manuel Piñeiro urged PCCh leader Luís Corvalán to establish a unified Chilean opposition.[239] Corvalán subsequently informed the PCC Congress in Havana of his party's new line, which called for "armed struggle" against the Pinochet dictatorship in coordination with the MIR and other extremist groups.[240] A Radio Moscow broadcast of March 2, 1985, transmitted the decisions of the PCCh's January 1985 Plenum to use all means, including armed violence, against the Pinochet regime and to support its "allied organization," the Manuel Rodríguez Popular Front (FPMR).[241] Experts generally regarded the FPMR as a terrorist front for the PCCh, at least until seventy percent of the FPMR allegedly broke away from the party in November 1986.[242]

In the mid-1980s, a systematic bombing campaign by the MIR and FPMR has plagued the Santiago area, causing frequent blackouts. Since 1982, U.S.-associated facilities in Chile have become the target of increasing bombing attacks (over two dozen). In 1984 alone, the FPMR perpetrated a claimed 735 bombings. In 1985, it began using remote-controlled car bombs as powerful

---

[238] State Dept., *Cuba's Renewed Support*, p. 11.

[239] "Castro meets with Chilean Communist Party official," *FBIS*, vol. 6, December 9, 1981, p. Q2.

[240] *Granma*, December 27, 1981, p. 1.

[241] "Situation in Chile," *Bulletin of the U.S. Department of State*, July 1985, p. 85.

[242] See, for example, Paul Sigmund's article on the PCCh in Richard F. Staar, ed., *Yearbook on International Communist Affairs 1986: Parties and Revolutionary Movements* (Stanford University, Stanford, California: Hoover Institution Press, 1986), pp. 64-66.

as fifty kilograms. From October 1984 through November 1985, it claimed responsibility for eleven car bombings, including one outside the U.S. consulate in Santiago in July 1985. On April 29, 1986, the FPMR exploded a 15-kilogram bomb at the U.S. ambassador's residence in Santiago to protest the U.S. air raid on Libya.[243]

Chilean terrorists carried out 1,729 bombings and incendiary attacks between January 1, 1985, and April 30, 1986. The bombing campaign escalated in 1984 following the clandestine return to Chile of Chilean extremists who had undergone training in Cuba, Nicaragua, and Libya.[244] At a world terrorist conference held in Managua in February 1986, MIR Secretary General Andrés Pascal Allende (Salvador Allende's nephew) requested facilities for the training of MIR members in Nicaragua, as an extension and supplement to those already existing in Cuba.[245]

The degree to which Cuba and the Soviet Union are committed to overthrowing the Pinochet government by "armed struggle" was revealed on August 6, 1986, when Chilean authorities discovered the first of ten FPMR arms caches, totaling seventy tons (the largest stash of weapons ever secretly amassed by extremists in a Latin American country). The Soviet equipment had been manufactured recently in Bulgaria; the U.S. weapons were traced, according to U.S. experts, to former U.S. stockpiles sent to South Vietnam in the late 1960s.[246] Some of the twenty-one individuals captured in connection with the FPMR arsenals, including four Cuban-trained FPMR members, told authorities of meetings in Nicaragua, training in Cuba, and months of preparation to receive the weapons, which arrived in two batches in July 1986.[247]

A State Department official confirmed that U.S. experts had positively

---

[243] *FBIS*, vol. 6, April 30, 1986, p. E1.

[244] "Situation in Chile," *Bulletin of the U.S. Department of State*, July 1985, p. 88.

[245] *El Mercurio* [Santiago], February 14, 1986, and September 21, 1986.

[246] *El Mercurio*, August 15, 16, 21, and 23, 1986, p. A1, and August 12, 1987, p. A1; and Shirley Christian, "Chile Arms Caches are Laid To Cuba," *New York Times*, October 19, 1986, p. 21.

[247] Bradley Graham, "Arms Caches in Chile Prompt Reassessment of Rebel Might," *Washington Post*, September 17, 1986.

established that Cuba sent the weapons.[248] According to Chilean officials, more than 200 individuals participated in transferring the weapons from Soviet and Cuban merchant or fishing ships into chartered Chilean fishing boats, and then in carrying them ashore in rubber dinghies (Zodiacs).[249] Chilean authorities also reported that Cuba, Nicaragua, and the Soviet Union provided $20 million through an International Guerrilla Coordinating Committee (CCGI) to finance the landing of weapons and explosives in the northern zone of Chile and the subsequent failed assassination attempt made by the FPMR against General Pinochet. In that action on September 7, 1986, fifteen FPMR terrorists attacked the General's motorcade with grenades and automatic weapons, killing five members of the presidential guard and wounding ten military escorts.[250]

According to Chile's director general of Investigative Police, both the FPMR and MIR receive urban guerrilla training in Cuba at the Punto Cero, Pinar del Rio, Trinidad, and Havana camps. The official added that Cuba provides logistical support, whereas the Soviet Union gives them financial and propaganda assistance, and other aid comes from Nicaragua and Libya.[251] Chile's Attorney General Ambrosio Rodríguez reported on January 22, 1988, that Cuban and Nicaraguan agents were commanding a newly created International Guerrilla Coordinating Board (presumably the CCGI) that had politically reunited the MIR and FPMR under Cuban command. He added that MIR and FPMR cadres were being trained in Cuba and East Germany.[252]

Bolivia

Cuba's reinvolvement in Bolivia, fifteen years after the Guevara fiasco, began formally in October 1982 when Cuban officials attended the presidential inauguration of Hernán Siles Zuazo. By late 1983, sixty to seventy Cuban

---

[248] Omang, *op cit,* citing Robert S. Gelbard, deputy assistant secretary of state for South American affairs.

[249] *El Mercurio*, August 28, 1986, p. A1; and Graham, *op cit.*

[250] "Special Report: The Terrorist Connections in Chile," *El Mercurio*, November 27, 1986, p. C7.

[251] *El Mercurio*, May 26, 1987, p. A1, 10, citing Chilean police official Fernando Paredes Pizarro.

[252] *FBIS*, vol. 6, January 27, 1988, p. 27, citing Santiago Domestic Service.

agents reportedly were operating in Bolivia, trying to build a support base among the smaller Marxist-Leninist groups and providing guerrilla training and weapons for their members.[253] The subversive efforts of the Cubans reportedly were being directed by DA official Angel Burgez (sic), the chargé d'affaires at the Cuban consulate in La Paz, and another DA agent, Manuel Basabe, a political counselor at the consulate.[254] The chargé d'affaires was actually Angel Brugues Pérez.[255] According to the Latin news media, Brugues has "vast experience in coordinating revolutionary activities" and was arrested in Brazil nine years earlier for smuggling machine-guns.[256] Revelations of Cuban subversive activities in Bolivia were reported in La Paz newspapers in 1983. One Bolivian arrested by the army affirmed that groups of fifteen to twenty Bolivians each were being flown by Cubana Airlines from Lima to Havana for three-month training programs in rural and urban guerrilla warfare at the "Comandante Ché" Camp, run by the MININT near Havana.[257] An unusual number of Cuban diplomatic couriers reportedly traveled from Lima to La Paz in 1984, carrying many crates immune to inspection.[258] In addition, DA "second chief" Armando Campos Ginesta visited La Paz twice in 1984. Ironically, the more conservative administration of Víctor Paz Estenssoro reestablished full diplomatic relations with Cuba in September 1988.

THE UNITED STATES

Puerto Rico

With the demise of U.S. radicals, Castro's surrogate terrorists in the United States have become Puerto Rican separatists. Puerto Rican terrorist groups

---

[253] Jay Mallin, Sr., "Cubans Find a Fertile Field for Subversion," *Washington Times*, March 2, 1984.

[254] *Ibid.*

[255] CIA, *Directory*, p. 223.

[256] "Cuban 'diplomatic couriers' seen sowing subversion in Latin America," *JPRS*, February 26, 1985, pp. 1-2, citing *El Tiempo* [Bogotá], November 27, 1984, which summarizes a press review in *La Estrella* [Panama], January 14, 1985, p. 11.

[257] "Guerrillas reportedly receiving training in Cuba," *FBIS*, vol. 6, August 22, 1983, pp. C1-C2, citing *El Diario* [La Paz], August 18, 1983.

[258] "Cuban 'diplomatic couriers'," *JPRS*, *op cit.*

were responsible for 55 percent of domestic terrorist group incidents in the United States during the 1980-86 period.[259] Many Puerto Rican extremists are known to have received terrorist training in Cuba. Dr. Daniel James testified before a U.S. Senate Subcommittee that the DGI, working through Filiberto Ojeda Ríos, organized the Armed Forces of National Liberation (FALN) in 1974.[260] Ojeda Ríos' association with the DGI actually began in 1961, according to a U.S. Senate Judiciary report.[261] In October 1974, he was arrested and charged with terrorist acts against American hotels in Puerto Rico. Authorities found a substantial amount of Cuban government documents and secret codes in his possession. He jumped bail soon thereafter, however, and disappeared for many years.[262] He was, however, credited with the 1979 unification of Puerto Rico's five principal terrorist groups into the Cuban-directed National Revolutionary Command (CRN).[263]

According to the former chief investigator of the U.S. Senate, Alfonso Tarabochia, the DA began directing terrorist activities in Puerto Rico and the eastern and midwestern United States as early as 1974.[264] That June, the secretary general of the Puerto Rican Socialist Party (PSP), Juan Marí Bras, met in Havana with Fidel Castro to consolidate party solidarity, according to testimony by a PSP specialist. Montané and Piñeiro also received the PSP delegation.[265] On January 26, 1973, the PSP opened its permanent offices in

---

[259] Federal Bureau of Investigation, *Analysis of Terrorist Incidents in the United States*, 1986 (1987), pp. 14, 53, and 56.

[260] Senate, *Role of Cuba, op cit*, p. 167.

[261] Senate, *The Castro Connection*, pp. 467-468.

[262] Diego A. Abich, "Puerto Rico's Struggle with Cuban-Supported Terrorism," *Wall Street Journal*, May 9, 1986, p. 27.

[263] Daniel James, "Puerto Rico's terrorists: a real threat to Reagan?" *Dallas Morning News*, December 27, 1981, p. G1.

[264] U.S. Congress, Senate, Committee on the Judiciary, Internal Security Subcommittee, *Terroristic Activity: The Castro Connection in Puerto Rico: Castro's Hand in Puerto Rican and U.S. Terrorism*, 94th Cong., 1st sess., Part 6, July 30, 1975, p. 379.

[265] See testimony of Francisco Martínez, a specialist in the PSP, in Senate, *The Cuban Connection*, pp. 355, 357.

Havana and, by 1974, was "operating as a branch of the Cuban intelligence and espionage apparatus."[266]

Beginning in September 1974, the incidence of terrorist bombings by Puerto Rican extremists, particularly the FALN, escalated sharply. Targets included U.S. companies and public places. For example, the FALN was responsible for a powerful blast that killed four patrons and wounded dozens at the historic Fraunces Tavern in lower Manhattan on January 25, 1975. Later that year, Castro sponsored the First World Solidarity Conference for the Independence of Puerto Rico in Havana. A day after the Second World Solidarity meeting, held in Mexico from November 30 to December 2, 1979, the Macheteros celebrated by machine-gunning a U.S. Navy bus in Sabana Seca, Puerto Rico, killing two sailors and seriously wounding ten others with AK-47 fire.

Since 1978, the Macheteros has been one of the most active of the more than half-dozen Puerto Rican terrorist groups. The Organization of Volunteers for the Puerto Rican Revolution (OVRP) also has claimed responsibility for several of the same attacks.[267] In January 1981, Macheteros commandos destroyed nine U.S. military jet fighters, worth $45 million, at the Muñiz Air National Guard Base in San Juan. (Cuban-trained Salvadoran FMLN commandos duplicated the action a year later in El Salvador.)

The FBI reported that the Macheteros, in attacks on federal buildings in Puerto Rico in 1983-85, used U.S.-made M-72 antitank weapons that were known to have been transferred by Vietnam to Cuba after the United States pulled out of the Vietnam war.[268] In an operation that the DA reportedly supported with training and weapons, the Macheteros robbed a Wells Fargo depot in Hartford, Connecticut, of $7.2 million on September 12, 1983. Federal authorities who were quoted by *Insight* magazine explained that following the heist, Macheteros leaders Ojeda Ríos and Jorge Farinacci García disagreed on how to distribute the money. Ojeda Ríos wanted to turn over all

---

[266] *Ibid.*, pp. 353,338.

[267] Karl Schoenberger, "Puerto Rican Group Vows New Attacks," *Hartford Courant*, November 8, 1985, p. 10.

[268] Ronald J. Ostrow, "Weapons Used by Terrorists Tied to Cuba," *Los Angeles Times*, September 4, 1985, p. 1.

of it to Cuba, whereas Farinacci insisted that at least $2.5 million remain in Puerto Rico; Faranacci's faction won out.[269] According to the FBI, $4 million from the theft was sent to Cuba and the operation's ringleader, Macheteros member Victor Manuel Gerena, employed as one of the Wells Fargo guards, was given sanctuary in Cuba.[270]

In September 1985, the FBI announced the capture in Puerto Rico of Ojeda Ríos and eleven reputed Macheteros members.[271] The U.S. indictment against Ojeda Ríos reportedly provides documentation that he and other Macheteros leaders maintained contact in Mexico with Fernando Comas, the DA official who coordinated the Sandinista guerrillas from the Cuban consulate in Costa Rica. The Macheteros leaders and Comas reportedly discussed what to do with the $7.2 million Wells Fargo loot.[272] After being held for thirty-two months in pretrial detention, Ojeda Ríos was released on $1 million bail in May 1988.

That June, the Mexican government placated the Castro regime but angered U.S. officials by releasing Ojeda's FALN comrade William "Guillermo" Morales from prison and putting him on a plane to Havana, where he was granted asylum. One of the most dangerous and fanatical of the Puerto Rican separatists, Morales had escaped from custody in New York in 1979 while serving ninety-nine years on terrorist bombing and murder charges and fled to Mexico, where he was captured after a gun battle in which he killed a policeman.

Having made the cause of Puerto Rican independence a priority of Cuban foreign policy for many years, Castro has a loyal following among the separatists. After an unexplained fifteen-year delay, Cuba "officially inaugurated" the PSP's permanent offices in the exclusive Miramar district of Havana in April 1987; Piñeiro and Montané received PSP Secretary General Carlos Gallisá Bisbal on that occasion, just as they had met with his predecessor in 1973.[273]

---

[269] Jerry Seper, "The Cuban Spark in Puerto Rico," *Insight*, February 2, 1987, p. 29.

[270] *AP*, "12 Arrested in 1983 Heist That Totaled $7 Million," *Washington Post*, August 31, 1985, p. A13.

[271] Ostrow, *op cit.*

[272] Abich, *op cit.*

[273] *Granma*, April 9, 1987, p. 2.

VIII. DA/DGRE FOREIGN POLICY INFLUENCE

Despite the central roles played by the DGRE and DA in Cuba's worldwide subversive program and foreign policies, and despite reports in *Granma* of important meetings held by these officials, Cubanologists generally have not devoted much attention to analyzing their roles and influence. Those analysts have long assumed, quite erroneously, that the overt, diplomatic side of Cuban foreign relations is all that needs to be examined in order to understand Cuba's foreign policy.

One of the few scholars in academia to at least note the existence of the DA and DGRE, Juan del Aguila, opined that they probably only implement and oversee policies made by the PCC's Politburo.[274] Although the DGRE and DA no doubt follow general policy guidelines set by the Politburo, they probably also have a significant role in formulating revolutionary policies that are appropriate to the particular conditions existing in a country or region, not to mention their important diplomatic as well as covert activities. After all, numerous Cuban ambassadors were previously identified as DA officials. The DGRE and DA, in effect, carry out Fidel Castro's covert foreign policy, the one that seeks to unify, coordinate, and support self-described anti-imperialist "national liberation movements" worldwide.

Juan Valdés Paz, an official of the DA's CEA, summed up that policy toward Latin America in a 1984 paper presented in Mexico City. Valdés stated that "...the foreign policy of the Cuban revolution has had as a permanent objective the achievement of unity in Latin America and the Caribbean, and has offered all its support to any action leading toward such unity."[275] This "unity" that Valdés was referring to was not the unity of Latin American nations. Rather, he stated explicitly and candidly that the permanent Cuban objective was the unity of "revolutionary movements." Such a policy is not formulated by the Ministry of Foreign Relations (MINREX), but by the PCC/CC's revolutionary support apparatus, namely the DGRE and DA. Foreign Minister Isodoro Malmierca performs only the ceremonial or traditional

---

[274] Juan M. del Aguila, "Revolution and Foreign Policy-making: How Cuba Influences Nicaragua," in Steven W. Hughes and Kenneth J. Mijeske, *Politics and Public Policy in Latin America* (Boulder: Westview, 1984), p. 166.

[275] Juan Valdéz Paz, "Cuba and the Crisis in Central America," *Contemporary Marxism* 10 (1985), p. 58.

diplomatic aspects of Cuban foreign policy, such as relations with Western states. The DA and DGRE chiefs normally meet with as many foreign leaders or representatives of foreign parties or groups as Malmierca does.

As DGRE chief or simply by virtue of his Politiburo membership, Jorge Risquet, unlike former DGRE chief Montané, may have some bureaucratic authority over the DA and Piñeiro. In some meetings that Risquet held with delegations from Latin American countries, the presence of Piñeiro was noted. DA officials other than Piñeiro also were present in meetings that Risquet has held with visitors from Latin America. For example, DA official José Fernández Vilela attended Risquet's meeting with the Uruguayan Labor Minister in November 1986. The DGRE also apparently has some bureaucratic representation in MINREX. For example, Granma identified Oscar Fernández Padilla as both vice minister of foreign relations and chief of section of the DGRE.[276]

Risquet greatly outranks Malmierca, but Piñeiro also appears to have considerably more influence with Fidel Castro on foreign affairs than does Malmierca. According to Castro biographer Tad Szulc, the post of DA chief is "one of the most powerful political positions."[277] In addition to serving as Castro's chief aide on Latin American revolutionary affairs, Piñeiro, also a PCC/CC member, is reported to be his key adviser on Cuban policy toward the United States.[278] Szulc has personally observed that Piñeiro, whose beard is now white, is invariably present at social functions held in the Palace of the Revolution, "usually standing near Castro with a small group of the top leadership," and "has permanent access to Castro's third-floor office."[279] Piñeiro's frequent meetings with visiting leaders of Latin American guerrilla and terrorist groups, CPs, and opposition parties or Socialist regimes are noted occasionally by the Cuban media. For example, Havana television reported that Piñeiro received Ecuadorean leftist politician Abdala Bucaram Ortiz at Havana's airport on May 20, 1988.[280]

---

[276] Granma, April 11, 1987, p. 95.

[277] Tad Szulc, Fidel: A Critical Portrait (New York: William & Morrow & Co., 1986), p. 617.

[278] As noted by Jim Hoagland in his interview with Castro, op cit.

[279] Szulc, p. 74.

[280] FBIS, vol. 6, May 23, 1988, p. 2.

According to Mallin, Piñeiro has approval authority over all diplomatic appointments in the hemisphere below the rank of minister-counselor, as well as the authority to appoint ambassadors in key countries.[281] Mallin mentioned, however, that DA official Pedro Silvio González Pérez was the minister-counselor in Georgetown, Guyana, which would suggest that the minister-counselor rank is also within Piñeiro's appointive powers. Mallin also has reported that DA officials are present in every Cuban diplomatic mission in Latin America and the Caribbean, as well as at the United Nations in New York. According to Mallin, every Cuban diplomatic post, as well as the Cuban Missions in Washington, D.C. and at the UN, has two or three DA officials, and in some key countries there are five or six agents.[282]

Aspillaga affirmed that DA officials occupy even the highest-level posts within Cuba's foreign diplomatic missions, and that at least half of the sixty-five to seventy Cubans assigned to the Cuban Mission at the U.N. and all Cubans assigned to the twenty-member Cuban Interests Section in Washington, D.C., are intelligence agents posing as diplomats.[283] DA officials have held ambassadorships in at least seven countries: Barbados, Colombia, Dominica, Jamaica, Nicaragua, Suriname, and St. Lucia. As the country profiles in this report demonstrate, DA ambassadorial appointments usually indicate that the host country is a special target for subversion by the Cubans. In the early 1980s, the subversive activities of DA operatives resulted in ruptures in Cuban diplomatic relations with Colombia, Costa Rica, Jamaica, and Suriname. None of these countries had re-established diplomatic relations with Cuba by October 1988.

IX. THE SOVIET-CUBAN DIPLOMATIC GAMBIT

As a result of Castro's considerable skills as an elder statesman and the DA's sophisticated, covert approach to supporting subversive activities in the Americas, many Latin American democratic leaders apparently are willing to believe that Cuba gave up exporting revolution in favor of reentering the Latin

---

[281] Jay Mallin, "Cuban Intelligence Elite Pushes Subversion in Americas," *Washington Times*, August 25, 1983, p. 7A.

[282] *Ibid.*

[283] Joe Pichirallo, "Cuba Used Noriega to Obtain High-Tech U.S. Goods, Defector Says," *Washington Post*, April 27, 1988, p. A24.

American community or have hoped that normalization of relations with Cuba will appease the left in their own countries.

Castro's opportunity to break out of the growing diplomatic isolation in which Cuba found itself in 1981 came with the 1982 Falkland/Malvinas Islands war between Argentina and Britain. While the United States backed Britain, Castro gained diplomatic support in Latin America by siding with Argentina. And despite Castro's humiliating setback in Grenada in October 1983, Cuba's diplomatic standing began to improve in 1985 as Bolivia and Uruguay restored full diplomatic relations with Cuba. Far more significantly, Brazil, the region's largest country, did the same in 1986. The DA could take some of the credit for Cuba's rapprochement with Brazil. DA agent Sergio Cervantes, in his capacity as an envoy of the Castro regime, is reported to have engaged in extensive lobbying of Brazilian government officials.[284] Brazil's Foreign Ministry, however, rejected Castro's appointment in August 1986 of a senior subversive agent, Colonel René Rodríguez Cruz, to serve as one of Cuba's two top diplomats in its future embassy in Brasilia after the *O Estado de São Paulo* newspaper published an incriminating photograph of Rodríguez. The photo, which was provided by Armando Valladares—a Cuban writer and former political prisoner—showed Rodríguez holding an automatic pistol and standing over the body of a man who apparently had just been "executed."[285] Valladares told the newspaper in an interview that Rodríguez, as ICAP director, is responsible for Cuba's intelligence operations abroad, and that Brazil ranked second only to Mexico as the most important country for Castro's subversive plans.

The Soviet regime of CPSU leader Mikhail Gorbachev began actively courting influential non-Marxist nations in Latin America in 1986—principally Argentina, Brazil, and Mexico, but also Panama and Uruguay.[286] Gorbachev's approach, however, appeared to differ little from the 1960s when the Soviets allowed the Cubans to support "armed struggle" in selected Latin American

---

[284] Olga Nazario, "Brazil's Rapprochement With Cuba: The Process and the Prospect," *Journal of Interamerican Studies & World Affairs*, vol. 28, no. 3 (Fall 1986), p. 78.

[285] See *O Estado de S. Paulo*, August 31, 1986, p. 1.

[286] Bill Keller, "Soviet, in a Shift, Expands Contact With Third World," *New York Times*, May 25, 1987.

countries of no diplomatic or trade interest for the Soviet Union, while Moscow pursued diplomatic and commercial objectives in the larger countries. "Favored" countries such as Mexico already have seen how the sizeable "diplomatic" presence of the Soviets, like the Cubans, can become an internal security threat.[287]

X. CONCLUSION AND OUTLOOK

Although the Monroe Doctrine promulgated in 1823 may now be obsolete, the principle of preventing extrahemispheric threats to this hemisphere has remained a fundamental tenet of both U.S. and inter-American security policies and interests during the 20th century. It is the basis of the Inter-American (Rio) Treaty on Reciprocal Military Assistance of 1947, which President Kennedy invoked in the 1962 missile crisis. Independently of any Monroe Doctrine, the prohibition against foreign interference in the hemisphere and the right to defend against it is recognized by international law and the UN Charter. The latter provides for regional defense arrangements such as those specified in the Rio Treaty and the OAS Charter. Just as the Cubans use Nicaragua and the various Marxist-Leninist groups as their proxies, the Soviet Union employs Cuba and the CPs as its surrogates. Thus, these surrogate forces within the region constitute, *ipso facto*, an extrahemispheric threat.

Isolating Cuba from its Nicaraguan and Soviet allies, not simply from the non-Communist countries, will be essential if the United States ever hopes to rectify its past policy mistakes and contain and eventually eliminate the threat posed by the Soviets' use of Cuba as a strategic platform and the fountainhead for subversion, guerrilla warfare, and terrorism in the hemisphere. Conversely, isolating Nicaragua from its Cuban, other Soviet bloc, and Libyan allies will be a prerequisite to dealing effectively with the Cuban problem. The growing Soviet bloc threat in Central America will inevitably develop into a strategic crisis for the Americas if the subversive and military efforts of Cuba and Nicaragua continue unchecked.

Indeed, anti-U.S. and anti-government Castroite terrorism in Latin America will likely increase and could very well spread to Panama. In May 1988, the FMLN vowed to launch a new terrorist campaign against Americans in El

---

[287] See, for example, "The Plot to Destroy Mexico," in Barron, *KGB*, pp. 312-348.

Salvador. The Sandinista regime is likely to fulfill the "robot" role assigned it by the Cubans. For example, in a July 1987 speech marking the eighth anniversary of the Sandinista takeover, President Daniel Ortega threatened that he might follow Castro's lead by providing arms to revolutionaries and terrorists in Haiti and Chile, as well as those in Puerto Rico.[288]

Weapons used by the Castroite groups will become increasingly sophisticated and lethal as foreign terrorist techniques and technologies are assimilated, with Cuban and Nicaraguan assistance. Nicaraguan defector Major Roger Miranda stated publicly on December 12, 1987, that Soviet and Cuban officials were planning to discuss the FMLN's request for SA-7 antiaircraft missiles at a meeting scheduled for mid-November 1987 in Havana. He added that, although the Nicaraguans were training fifteen FMLN guerrillas to use the shoulder-fired missiles, Nicaraguan Defense Minister Humberto Ortega preferred that the Cubans handle the transfer of the weapons to the FMLN.[289] When Duarte confronted Daniel Ortega with the charge in mid-January 1988, the Nicaraguan leader threatened to provide the SA-7 missiles to the FMLN if the U.S. Congress approved new aid to the Contras.[290]

Castroite terrorism can be expected to revisit Puerto Rico in coming years. In 1987, according to federal authorities, Puerto Rican terrorists—funded by $4 million in proceeds from the Wells Fargo robbery—were reportedly undergoing extensive training in Cuba and Nicaragua in preparation for a new wave of violence. The expected targets included U.S. military personnel and equipment in Puerto Rico, as well as federal and local law enforcement authorities working there. Cubans and Nicaraguans were believed to be operating the training camps, but Libyans and Bulgarians also were suspected of providing some of the training.[291]

Given Cuba's current targets of opportunity in Colombia, Panama, and

---

[288] *Washington Times*, August 10, 1987.

[289] Joe Pichirallo and Terri Shaw, "Top Defector Disillusioned By Marxism," *Washington Post,* December 13, 1987, p. A1.

[290] Josette Shiner, "Ortega Levels Missile Threat At El Salvador," *Washington Times*, January 29, 1988, p. A1.

[291] Jerry Seper, "Managua Aids Puerto Rican Terror Schools," *Washington Times*, January 13, 1987.

Central America, Castro is not likely to launch a terrorist campaign in the continental United States anytime soon without a significant pretext, such as U.S. military action against Nicaragua. If that happened, according to Miranda, Cuban and Nicaraguan forces would also try to "regionalize" the conflict in Central America by carrying out military operations against Nicaragua's neighbors and U.S. facilities in the region, including capturing U.S. personnel and property and destroying the U.S. embassy in San José, Costa Rica. In any event, Castro clearly intends to continue using the Latin American and Puerto Rican Marxist-Leninist groups as well as his Nicaraguan "robot" to wage his surrogate terrorist war against the Americas.

APPENDIX 1

CITED DA OFFICIALS

Arbesú Fraga, José Antonio	A vice chief
Abreu Quintana, Ramiro	Chief, Central American Section
Arteaga Hernández, Damian	First Secretary, Buenos Aires
Bassols Suárez, Gonzalo	Former First Secretary, Bogotá
Brugues Pérez, Angel	Chargé d'Affaires, La Paz
Barahona López, Andrés (aka "Renán Montero Corrales")	Chief, Nicaragua's Fifth Directorate of Intelligence
Cabrera, Roberto	A section chief
Campos Ginesta, Armando	A vice chief
Cárdenas Junquera, Oscar Osvaldo	Former Cuban Ambassador, Suriname
Carranza Valdés, Julio	A CEA official
Cervantes, Sergio	Brazil Desk
Comas Pérez, Fernando Pascual	A CEAL official
Cordova Rivas, Omar Ramón	Caribbean Section Chief
Díaz Evarista, Gastón	Served in Grenada
Díaz Larrañaga, Carlos Andrés	Killed in Grenada
Estrada Fernández, Armando Ulises	A former vice chief
Fernández Vilela, José	An official
Fernández de Oña, Luís	A Section chief
García Almeida, Alfredo	Chief, North American Section
González Piñeiro, Pedro ("Justo")	An Advisor
González Pérez, Pedro Silvio	Minister-Counselor, Georgetown
Hernández Curbelo, Norberto	Ambassador to Nicaragua
Hernández Ojeda, Luís	Cuban Chargé d'Affaires, Managua
Hernández, Rafael	Director, CEA's United States Research Department
López Diáz, Julián	Former Ambassador to Managua
Ojalvo, José Luís	An official
Piñeiro Losada, Manuel	Chief, DA
Ravelo Renedo, Fernando	A vice chief

Ross Paz, José Francisco	Chargé d'Affaires, Quito
Suárez Salazar, Luís	Director, CEA
Valdés Paz, Juan	A CEA official
Villar Martínez, Ilya Felicia	Director, CEAL

APPENDIX 2
BIOGRAPHICAL PROFILE

Manuel Piñeiro Losada
(*"Barba Roja"*—Red Beard)

As chief of the DA and a member of the PCC/CC, Piñeiro is responsible for developing and implementing Cuba's political-military revolutionary program in the Americas. The son of a bar owner in Matanzas Province, Piñeiro probably was born in the 1920s. He is said to be a nephew of Cuba's Communist poet Nicolas Guillén.

Piñeiro studied business administration at Columbia University in New York in the early 1950s and was married to an American ballet dancer, Lorna Nell Burdsall, whom he later divorced. The bearded Piñeiro has been described by Jay Mallin as tall and slim, with "a hard, raucous voice." He joined Fidel Castro's 26th of July Movement and served in a column of Raúl Castro's Second Front. After Castro took power, Major Piñeiro was named chief of the Army in Oriente Province. Castro hand-picked him to serve on the Revolutionary Tribunals, formed to convict forty-three pilots and airmen guilty of "genocide." As one of Castro's most loyal supporters, Piñeiro became vice minister of the MININT in the autumn of 1959. That September he and G-2 chief Raúl Valdés Menéndez, whom he subsequently replaced, met with KGB official Vadim Kotchergine. In the early 1960s, according to Juan Vivés, a former Cuban security official, Piñeiro belonged to Valdés Menéndez's Fifth Bureau, which was composed of a small group of Cubans (whose identities were secret) and a large number of KGB advisers. In those days, Piñeiro was almost always accompanied by a KGB official named "Ivan."

By 1962 Piñeiro was chief of the newly established DGI. The Soviets forced him out of the position in 1968, however, because of his loyalty to Castro and his role in thwarting a KGB/PCC conspiracy to oust Castro. The grateful Cuban leader then appointed Piñeiro head of Cuba's National Liberation Directorate (DLN). In November 1974, Piñeiro was named DA chief, a position that he has held since then. A close adviser and confidant of Fidel Castro, Piñeiro is known to be audacious and smart.

[Sources: see Paul D. Bethel, *The Losers* (New Rochelle, N.Y.: Arlington House, 1969), p. 93; John Dorschner and Roberto Fabricio, *The Winds of December* (New York: Coward, McCann & Geoghegan, 1980), p. 115; Carlos Alberto Montaner, *Secret Report on the Cuban Revolution* (New Brunswick: Transaction Books, 1981), p. 186; Szulc, *Fidel*, p. 72; Thomas, *Cuban Revolution*, p. 144, 495 (fn); Juan Vives, p. 103; and Jay Mallin, "How Cuba Turned to Spies, Terror," *Washington Times*, August 23, 1983, p. A1.]

BOOK REFERENCES

Barron, John. *KGB: The Secret Work of Soviet Secret Agents*. New York: Bantam Books, 1974.

Bethel, Paul D. *The Losers*. New Rochelle, N.Y.: Arlington House, 1969.

Castro Hidalgo, Orlando. *Spy For Fidel*. Miami: E.A. Seeman Publishing, Inc., 1971.

Dobson, Christopher and Ronald Payne. *The Carlos Complex*. London: Coronet Books, 1977.

Dorschner, John and Roberto Fabricio. *The Winds of December*. New York: Coward, McCann & Geoghegan, 1980.

Falk, Pamela S. *Cuban Foreign Policy: Caribbean Tempest*. Lexington, Mass.: Lexington Books, 1986.

Fauriol, Georges, ed. *Latin American Insurgencies*. Washington, D.C.: Georgetown University Center for Strategic and International Studies, 1985.

Franqui, Carlos. *Diary of the Cuban Revolution*. New York: Viking Press, 1980.

Halperin, Maurice. *The Taming of Fidel Castro*. Berkeley: University of California Press, 1981.

Matthews, Herbert L. *Fidel Castro*. New York: Simon & Shuster, 1970.

_____. *Revolution in Cuba*. New York: Charles Scribner's Sons, 1975.

Moss, Robert. *Chile's Marxist Experiment*. Newton Abbot: David & Charles, 1973.

Ratliff, William E. *Castroism and Communism in Latin America, 1959-1976*. Washington/Stanford: AEI-Hoover Policy Studies, 1976.

Robbins, Carla Anne. *The Cuban Threat*. Philadelphia: ISHI Publications, 1985.

Sterling, Claire. *The Terror Network*. New York: Holt, Rinehart, & Winston, 1981.

Suarez, Andres. *Cuba: Castroism and Communism 1959-1966*. Cambridge, Mass.: MIT Press, 1967.

Szulc, Tad. *Fidel: A Critical Portrait*. New York: William Morrow & Company, 1986.

Thomas, Hugh. *The Cuban Revolution*. New York: Harper & Row Publishers, 1977.

Vivés, Juan. *Les Maitres du Cuba*. Paris: Robert Laffont, 1981.

Recent Titles by the Cuban American National Foundation:

Political Hospitality and Tourism: Cuba and Nicaragua, by Paul Hollander. This 32-page study exposes a systematic campaign of "political hospitality and tourism" designed to persuade elite groups of the virtues of the Fidelista and Sandinista Revolutions. Dr. Hollander is author of *Political Pilgrims: Travels of Western Intellectuals to the Soviet Union, China, and Cuba* (1981, 1983). Price: $4.00

Fidel Castro and the United States Press, by John P. Wallach. The essay explores how the American media has often given Castro the benefit of the doubt. It includes numerous examples of Castro's techniques in dealing with the media. John P. Wallach is the Foreign Affairs Editor for Hearst Newspapers. Price. $4.00

Castro's Puerto Rico Obsession is a study of Castro's campaign to promote a Marxist Puerto Rico. It details Castro's efforts to promote Puerto Rican "independence" in the United Nations and his support for Puerto Rican terrorist groups. Price: $4.00

General Del Pino Speaks: An Insight into Elite Corruption and Military Dissension in Castro's Cuba. An abridged translation of Radio Martí's 1987 interview with the highest ranking military officer ever to defect from Cuba. Topics include Cuba's involvement in Angola; corruption in the Cuban government; and the disillusionment among the Cuban people with the Castro regime. Price: $5.00.

Towards A New U.S.-Cuba Policy (1988). A briefing on Cuban domestic and international policies which offers thirty policy options for a new and more effective U.S. policy towards the Castro regime. Price: $4.00

The Cuban University Under the Revolution, by Eusebio Mujal-León. This 65-page essay examines the role of the university - the historic focal point of the Cuban struggle for independence and democracy - in the Cuba of Fidel Castro. Price: $5.00

Narco-Terrorism and the Cuban Connection, by Rachel Ehrenfeld. An analysis of Havana's role as "command center" for a network of narco-traffickers and terrorists in the Western Hemisphere. Price: $4.00

A Public Survey on the Quality of Health Care in the Province of Holguin, Cuba. A Confidential Report by the Cuban Communist Party. Smuggled out of Cuba and translated by the Cuban American National Foundation, this report effectively demolishes the myth of "great accomplishments" by Cuba in the field of health care. Price: $5.00